Dr. History's
SAMPLER

More Stories of California's Past

For Marilyn —

Thanks for
Sharing Danielle
as a student
of this beloved
Subject!

Dr. History's
SAMPLER

More Stories of California's Past

by

JIM RAWLS

Edited by
Leonard Nelson
and
Denise Culver Nelson

Illustrations by
Walt Stewart

McGraw-Hill, Inc.
New York St. Louis San Francisco Auckland Bogotá Caracas
Lisbon London Madrid Mexico Milan Montreal New Delhi
Paris San Juan Singapore Sydney Tokyo Toronto

Illustrations and Cover Design	*Walt Stewart*
Interior Design and Electronic Composition	*Leonard Nelson and Denise Nelson*
Copyediting and Proofreading	*Donna Kruger*
Senior Editor	*Julie Kehrwald*

DR. HISTORY'S
SAMPLER
MORE STORIES OF CALIFORNIA'S PAST

1234567890 MAL MAL 909876543

Rawls, James J.
    Dr. History's sampler : more stories of California's past /
by Jim Rawls
       p. 113 cm.
    Includes bibliographic references and index.
    Summary: A collection of easy-to-read stories from California's
    past, bringing out aspects of the state's history, ethnicity, culture,
    and geography.
    ISBN 0-07-051482-8 : $12.95
    1. California History-History-Juvenile literature.   [1.
California-
History.]   1. Title.   II. Title: Doctor History's sampler.

Printed in the United States of America by
Malloy Lithographing, Inc.

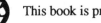

For

Phyllis L. Peterson

and all those who share
her love for lifelong learning

FOREWORD

Frank Dill and Mike Cleary
Morning Hosts for Dr. History's flagship radio station,
KNBR 680, San Francisco

The "man who makes history fun" is at it again. *Dr. History's Sampler* is another winning collection of stories drawn from California's colorful, spirited past.

A compelling advertising slogan for this book might be "Bet you can't read just one!" You see, reading one of Dr. History's fascinating episodes from either the *Whizz-Bang* or the *Sampler* is like trying to eat one potato chip. You can't do it. This is because Professor Jim Rawls possesses that rare talent for making an interesting subject FUN!

Take, for instance, his whimsical approach to story titles. Here the professor is downright mischievous! He puts just enough ambiguity in them to make for a good guessing game. When we spotted the story "W.C. Fields Forever," we thought the Beatles must be recording again. How about "Ebenezer and the *Otter?*" Could it be a sequel to Dickens' *A Christmas Carol?* Well, you'll have to turn to page eighteen to find out.

Those of you who have already enjoyed the good professor's first book know what wear and tear these books endure. So here's a tip for you first time readers: Buy several! In fact, buy many! This way, like reading glasses, you can leave some scattered about the house. One dog-eared, food-stained copy is hardly presentable. You'll also want to salt a few away as gifts for your history-deprived friends.

Another tip is to listen faithfully to the Frank and Mike Show on KNBR 680. It's here the stories of Dr. History are presented twice weekly by Jim Rawls himself. Which gives me an idea. Maybe--like those copies of the *Sampler* you're going to scatter about the house--you might leave a few radios tuned to.... Well, perhaps that's asking too much!

Frank Dill   Mike Cleary

PREFACE

In a world not so long ago, before our lives were filled with the countless diversions that keep us in a constant state of hyperactivity, folks passed the time with simpler pleasures. Stories were told and yarns were swapped by grownups on long winter's evenings, while children contented themselves with homemade toys fashioned from scraps of wood and calico.

Some of the most charming bits of Americana from those bygone days are *samplers*, winsome samples of needlework filled with scrolling letters and primitive images of hearth and home. Samplers were the special province of young girls who were taught by their mothers not only to use a needle skillfully but also to discover the joys of finishing a task thoroughly and well. Some samplers included aphorisms to warn the unwary:

Whistling girls and crowing hens
Always come to some bad ends.

Samplers often displayed all the stitches a girl knew, from basic cross stitches to the intricacies of double herringbones and fancy featherstitches. To see them now is to enter a world far different from our own, a world of simple beauty when there was time enough to be still and unhurried.

Samplers have been lovingly collected and displayed over the years, and their designs have been incorporated into a variety of products. Probably their most familiar use today is on the box of chocolates, first introduced in 1912, that offers a tantalizing invitation to partake of all the scrumptious assortment of chocolates inside, from the creamiest caramels to the crunchiest pecan clusters. A "sampler" is also what your waiter presents at the end of a fine meal, tempting you with such delicacies as *tiramisu*, some decadent chocolate mousse, or a slice of cheesecake drizzled with fresh blueberries.

Dr. History's Sampler: More Stories of California's Past continues this grand tradition of offering a wide assortment of treats...some of which may even keep you in stitches! You'll find here stories scattered throughout the Golden State, from the San Diego home of "The Purple Mother" to the northern ports of call of "California's Scandinavian Navy." The chronology ranges from the first Californians who lived in "aka L.A." to those today who know and celebrate the "Low-down on Lodi." There are tales here of famous visitors such as "Kipling the Kibitzer" and infamous residents like "The Bad Men of Bodie."

The marvelous diversity of California is here in all its glory, from the Bavarian-born merchant who invented "The Jeans that Won the West" to the African American who starred in "The Allensworth Story." Here too are stories of Danish Americans who came in search of "A Sunny Field and Pea Soup" and Japanese Americans who wondered "Is This Trip Necessary?"

The history of California *is* a sampler. It offers us an incredible abundance of stories to be savored and enjoyed, stories of remarkable color and texture. The emphasis in *Dr. History's Sampler* is on those stories that are comic, but a few are included to remind us of the tragic as well. The stories are short and lively, perfect for telling on a long winter's evening. As you read these stories--and consider all the fine stitchery that went into the making of our history--perhaps you'll find here something of your own story too.

ACKNOWLEDGMENTS

Without the help of many friends, this book could never have been written. Three individuals served with great distinction as research assistants and to them I am most grateful: Catherine Relf Ivers, Gillian H. Boeve, and Marlene Smith-Baranzini. Many of the best ideas and images in this book are theirs.

It is also a pleasure to acknowledge once again the support of my friends at the California Historical Society, especially Executive Director Michael McCone and Deputy Director Larry Campbell.

More than any other single individual, I am indebted to Dr. Phyllis L. Peterson, President of Diablo Valley College, for the continued success of Dr. History. She has been a constant source of encouragement and inspiration, reassuring me that broadcasting history on the radio is a logical extension of my teaching history in the classroom. It is to her that this book is dedicated with deep appreciation. Likewise I am most grateful to my friend Grant Cooke, Public Relations Officer for Diablo Valley College, for his enthusiastic support.

Not many commercial radio stations can boast that they offer a history feature during the morning commute hours--along with the news, sports, and weather--but such has been the proud claim of Dr. History's flagship station, KNBR 680, San Francisco. Credit for this innovation in programming is due to Vice President and General Manager Tony Salvadore, Manager of Station Administration Dwight Walker, and, especially, Operations Manager/Program Director Bob Agnew. Thank you, gentlemen, for your faith in the value (entertainment and otherwise) of history.

Frank Dill and Mike Cleary, the stars of KNBR's Frank & Mike Show, have been unwavering in their support of the Dr.

History feature. (And their test scores have showed steady improvement, a clear sign that they've been paying better attention in class!)

The producer of the show, Leonard Nelson, is the creator of Dr. History and continues to be its greatest champion. His editorial skills, and those of Denise Culver Nelson, are evident on every page of this book.

CONTENTS

ARF! THE GREAT SEAL

When the delegates to the California constitutional convention assembled in Monterey in 1849 they had several weighty items on their agenda. They needed to determine the official boundaries of California and the structure of its government. Perhaps the most pressing issue was whether to petition Congress for admission as a territory or as a state. Because the gold rush had already brought in such a large population, the delegates understandably resolved to skip the territorial stage and apply immediately for statehood.

One of the less earth-shaking decisions of the convention was to adopt an official state seal. Somewhat cluttered in design, the seal is filled with symbols of the new Golden State. The miner with his pick and shovel represents mineral wealth, the sheaf of wheat and bunch of grapes symbolize agriculture, and the ships stand for commerce. The Greek motto "Eureka" is a reminder of that historic day when Jim Marshall made his discovery at Sutter's Mill and *might* have said, "I have found it!" The thirty-one stars along the top symbolize California's desired status as the nation's thirty-first state. The seated figure with her plumed helmet and shield is Minerva, the Roman goddess of political wisdom and the guardian of cities. She was chosen to represent California because of her peculiar origins. As you no doubt recall from your study of classical mythology (right?), she sprang fully grown from the brow of her father Jupiter. Thus she was a perfect symbol for an "instant state," one seeking admission to the union without first being a territory.

The most controversial part of the seal is the grizzly bear standing at Minerva's side. This was the same symbol that had appeared on the Bear Flag, raised some three years earlier in Sonoma. One of the delegates at the convention was Mariano Guadalupe Vallejo, a proud *Californio* who had been captured and imprisoned by the Bear Flaggers. Vallejo was incensed to see that bear on the state seal. It should be removed, he thundered, or replaced by one with a rope around its neck and a *vaquero* yanking on the other end!

Now you may want to commit this little story to memory, or keep a copy of *Dr. History's Sampler* in the glove compartment of your car. You'll be glad you did the next time you're pulled over by the California Highway Patrol and look out your window and see the Great Seal of the State of California on the officer's gold badge. That might be the perfect time for a little diversionary conversation. Pointing to that luminous emblem, you might begin, "Excuse me, officer, did you know you've got a little Minerva on your badge?"

Something More ... Visit the site of the California Constitutional Convention at the Colton Hall Museum, City of Monterey, located on Pacific Street, between Jefferson and Madison, Monterey 93940. Free. Hours are 10:00 A.M. to 5:00 P.M. daily. Closed holidays. Telephone (408) 646-3851. One of the best places to see the Great Seal of the State of California is on the western steps of the state capitol located on Tenth Street, between L and N streets, Sacramento 95814.

THE JEANS THAT WON THE WEST

One of the most familiar names in all of California history is that of a Bavarian-born dry-goods merchant who arrived in the Golden State in 1853. He brought with him a load of canvas he hoped to sell to the gold miners for tents. But this merchant soon found a better use for his canvas, making pants for the miners. The merchant's name was Levi Strauss. (Actually his first name was "Loeb," but at some point he took the nickname of "Levi." A good thing, too, otherwise we'd all be walking around today wearing our "Loeb's.")

After his canvas ran out, Strauss switched to a tougher fabric that originated in Nimes, a town in the south of France. The cloth was called *serge de Nimes*, which later evolved into the more familiar "denim." Strauss used indigo to dye the cloth a deep blue. When miners complained that the weight of their gold nuggets caused the pockets to rip, Strauss and his partner in 1873 solved that problem by adding copper rivets. And there you have it, all the essentials of your modern-day 501s.

Stories about the strength and durability of Levi Strauss' famous pants became part of the folklore of the West. One young woman, mauled by a bear in Yosemite National Park, credited her Levi's with protecting her from serious injury. According to another account, a trainload of lumber heading to Flagstaff, Arizona, suddenly lost a coupling that held the cars to the engine. The engineer saved the day by taking off his Levi's, dousing them in water, twisting them into a rope, and tying the train back together!

Over the years, Levi Strauss & Company has made a few minor changes in the pants' basic design. In 1936 the company added a little red tab to the back pocket. It was also in the thirties that the name changed. The pants had been known as "waist-high overalls," but then the name "jeans" became more common. This new name was derived from the cotton trousers

worn by sailors from Genoa. (From *Genoese* comes "jeans.")
A more recent design change was suggested by none other than
the president of the company himself, Walter Haas, Sr. While
crouching around a roaring campfire, Haas discovered personally
what cowboys had always known. The rivet at the bottom of
his fly became a little too hot! And so, by executive order, that
particular rivet was banished forever from all future generations
of Levi's.

*Something More ... Visit the Levi Strauss Museum, 250 Valencia
Street, San Francisco 94103. Open by appointment only for groups.
To make arrangements for a tour, telephone (415) 565-9153. The best
account of Levi Strauss and his famous pants is Sondra Henry,*
Everyone Wears his Name *(1990).*

CALIFORNIA'S SCANDINAVIAN NAVY

Scandinavians have long been a part of the colorful history of the Golden State. Danes, Finns, Norwegians and Swedes have all contributed to California's multicultural past.

A Norwegian immigrant named John Thompson came to California in 1851 to mine gold. He didn't have much luck as a miner, but he soon recognized the need for someone to carry the mail across the Sierra Nevada. Thompson built himself a pair of skis--what he called "snowshoes"--and began transporting as much as a hundred pounds of mail a trip. He kept at it for twenty years and became famous throughout the West as "Snowshoe" Thompson.

Perhaps the best known Finn in California history was Gustave Niebaum, a retired seal hunter who settled in the Napa Valley and founded Inglenook Vineyards. Another enterprising Scandinavian was Peder Sather, a successful San Francisco banker whose name should be familiar to every Old Blue. After he died in 1886 his widow donated a couple of memorial gifts to the University of California at Berkeley: Sather Gate, standing near the southern entrance to the campus, and Sather Tower, better known today as the Campanile.

Several towns in California also have Scandinavian connections. Solvang in Santa Barbara County was founded by a group of Danish professors and ministers back in 1911, and the town of Turlock in Stanislaus County was a Swedish agricultural colony in the early 1900s.

Perhaps Scandinavians were best known for their role in the state's shipping industry. Scandinavian seamen were so numerous a century ago that they were called California's Scandinavian Navy. The rosters of captains and crews were filled with names like Nelson and Hansen, Peterson and Olsen. To avoid confusion, it became necessary to use nicknames. There was "Flatfoot" Hansen, "Swell Head" Nelson, and "Pie Face" Johnson.

Behind every nickname was a great story. "Rain Water" Johnson supposedly got his name by navigating his ship for two blocks *inland* on rain water before he realized his mistake! Then there was the story of Jack Bostrom. He was the captain of a lumber schooner that ran along the northern California coast. Apparently Capt'n Bostrom loved to party and always managed to maneuver his ship into port on Saturday night for the big country dances at Fort Bragg. His nickname was a natural, "Saturday Night" Jack.

My favorite tale from the days of California's Scandinavian Navy is about a fellow named "Hog" Aleck, the master of a steam schooner that sank in a terrific gale while carrying a cargo of pigs. When Aleck was being rescued, he shouted to his would-be saviors, "De hell mit me! You safe dem hogs!"

Something More ... Visit the San Francisco Maritime National Historical Park and Maritime Museum, 890 Beach Street at Polk, San Francisco 94109. Free. Telephone (415) 556-3002. Open 10:00 A.M. to 5:00 P.M. daily. A good book on the Scandinavian Navy of the Golden State is Jack McNairn and Jerry MacMullen, Ships of the Redwood Coast *(1945).*

THE PURPLE MOTHER

No, this is not the story of the dear old Mom of "The Purple People Eater" made famous by pop singer Sheb Wooley in 1957. "The Purple Mother" was the affectionate title given to a remarkable Californian named Katherine Tingley, a woman who just happened to be partial to the color purple. Founder of a utopian colony at San Diego's Point Loma in 1897, she once was described as "a vigorous woman, with a stout frame, dark hair and gray, restless eyes." When she was in her late thirties, she converted to a mystical movement known as "theosophy" that embraced the universal brotherhood of humanity as well as the doctrine of reincarnation. She soon became a leader of the movement and was quite successful in attracting wealthy investors, including the great manufacturer of sports equipment, Albert G. Spalding, famous for his basketballs and golf clubs.

Katherine Tingley ran a tight ship at Point Loma. All the men wore uniforms, while the women wore simple, almost identical dresses. Children lived in separate dormitories called

"lotus homes" and generally saw their parents only on weekends. Visitors were impressed by the strict order and discipline; a lot of saluting always seemed to be going on. But under the Purple Mother's leadership, the colony did flourish. She oversaw the construction of some forty buildings, including three that were topped with aquamarine and purple-colored domes. The colony also produced much of its own food, and even contributed to California's agricultural development with its cultivation of the avocado.

The press had a field day with some of the theosophists' more outlandish beliefs and practices. It was widely reported, for instance, that Katherine Tingley believed her dog Spot was her reincarnated husband. The *Los Angeles Times* mocked the colony as "the spookery" and charged that the Purple Mother ruled her followers with a "strange hypnotic power." The *Times* also published lurid accounts of late-night, co-ed pilgrimages by the colonists in their bathrobes, and the practice of "gross immoralities" by the sea. A local minister called upon all upstanding citizens of San Diego to denounce this shameless behavior.

The Point Loma colony disbanded a few years after Katherine Tingley's death in 1929. Today it's just a faded memory. But perhaps the next time you chip to the green with your Spalding pitching wedge, or dip your tortilla chip into some luscious guacamole, you'll pause for a moment to remember this tale of the Purple Mother.

Something More ... Visit the site of the Point Loma colony, now home to the Point Loma Nazarene College, 3900 Lomaland Drive, San Diego 92106. Free. Telephone (619) 221-2200. College officials will be happy to direct you to a number of the original buildings, including the only remaining lotus home. Read about the colony in Emmett Greenwalt, California Utopia: Point Loma *(1978) and Robert Hine,* California's Utopian Colonies *(1966).*

ON THE LAM

Not all the folks who came to California during the gold rush came to look for gold. Some were "on the lam," trying to escape their unsavory pasts. Back then, if you knew what was good for you, you didn't poke around in other people's business and inquire about their past. This code of mutual anonymity was spoofed in a popular gold rush ballad:

Oh, what was your name in the States?
Was it Thompson or Johnson or Bates?
Did you murder your wife and flee for your life?
Oh, What was your name in the States?

Violations of the code rarely went unpunished. James King of William, the oddly named crusading editor of the *San Francisco Bulletin*, paid dearly for publishing an exposé in 1856 about county supervisor James P. Casey. King maintained that the pen was not only mightier than the sword, but that the printing press was a mightier punishment of evil than the gallows. It was his mission, he firmly believed, to shed light on what others believed should remain hidden. Editor King revealed that prior to coming to California, Supervisor Casey had served time in the New York state penitentiary at Sing Sing. Casey was so outraged by this embarrassing revelation that he stormed into the offices of the *Bulletin* and demanded a retraction from King. An hour later, he shot and mortally wounded King on the streets of San Francisco. Casey was arrested by the city's Vigilance Committee, given a quick trial, and publicly hanged outside the second-story windows of the vigilantes' headquarters on Front and Davis streets.

Another infamous case of exposure involved a fellow known as Talbot H. Green. He was a wealthy and well-respected San Franciscan who was honored by having his name

bestowed on one of the city's main thoroughfares. In 1851 he decided to run for mayor. Then, while attending an elegant fancy-dress ball, a woman approached and addressed him as "Paul Geddes." As it turns out, this was indeed his real name. Geddes had fled his former life as a bank robber in Philadelphia and escaped to San Francisco with his loot. Needless to say, the dance ended in an uproar and so, too, did Paul Geddes' political career. But that street in the city by the Bay still bears his alias, San Francisco's Green Street.

Something More ... Read the story of Talbot Green, nee Paul Geddes, and other fascinating Californians in Doris Muscatine's delightful Old San Francisco: The Biography of a City *(1975). The dramatic story of early California journalism and politics is found in John Bruce,* Gaudy Century *(1948).*

HANGTOWN FRY

Here's a little quiz for you to try on your friends. What do Studebakers, Armour Star Wieners, and Hangtown Fry all have in common? You're sure to stump 'em unless they're up on their history of the little gold rush town of Placerville in El Dorado County.

Placerville started out in 1848 as a mining camp called Dry Diggings. It was only a few miles from the spot where Jim Marshall discovered gold at Sutter's Mill, and so the nearby ravines and hillsides were soon filled with eager miners. Some of the folks who settled in these parts were pretty rough characters, including a few who were publicly whipped for their misdeeds. Other less fortunate rascals were hanged from a tall tree on Main Street. For a while the town proudly bore the nickname of Hangtown. Only later, after things settled down a bit, was it renamed Placerville.

Several of Placerville's leading citizens went on to great fame and fortune. Mark Hopkins and Collis P. Huntington were local hardware merchants who moved to Sacramento on their way to becoming railroad barons and half of the illustrious Big Four. In the 1850s, a young blacksmith named John M. Studebaker opened a shop on Main Street and did a brisk business building wheelbarrows for the miners. Later he returned to Indiana, where he and his brothers became the world's leading manufacturers of wagons and buggies. Eventually they went on to build automobiles, and from 1902 until 1963 the streets and highways of America were graced with sleek, new (you guessed it!) Studebakers.

Another up-and-coming Placerville merchant was a butcher from New York named Philip Danforth Armour. He made a small fortune cutting meat during the gold rush and then went back to Chicago where he and his family became multi-millionaires running the largest meat-packing business in the world. One of its most popular creations, consumed all across the land today, is the Armour Star Wiener.

Perhaps Placerville's greatest claim to fame is its contribution to the culinary arts. According to local legend, back in 1849 a miner from nearby Shirttail Bend once sauntered into the Cary House in Placerville, plunked down a bag of gold nuggets, and asked for the most expensive meal on the menu. The cook replied that oysters and eggs were the two most pricey items. The miner told the cook to mix 'em together and serve 'em up. The resulting concoction--sort of a fried oyster omelette--became popular throughout the mother lode and is known to this day as Hangtown Fry.

Something More ... A great time to visit Placerville is in June during the annual Hangtown Pioneer Days when an authentic wagon train arrives in town at the El Dorado County Fairgrounds, 100 Placerville Drive, Placerville 95667. Telephone (916) 626-4990. The story of the gold rush is wonderfully told in J.S. Holliday, The World Rushed In *(1981).*

aka L.A.

Whenever I think about the early days of Los Angeles, I'm struck by several observations that foreshadowed the city's later history. When Juan Rodríguez Cabrillo sailed along the coast in 1542, he found the air so hazy from Indian campfires that he named the place *El Bahía de los Fumos* ("the Bay of Smokes"). Later, when Captain Gaspar de Portolá led the first Spanish expedition through the Los Angeles basin in 1769, he discovered it was more densely populated than other parts of California. Some 5,000 Gabrielino Indians were living in twenty-eight separate villages. Captain Portolá also felt the earth move. He recognized the deep rumblings in the earth for what they were, and thus he named a nearby river *El Rio de los Temblores* ("the River of the Temblors"). So even before the city was founded, several key elements of its later development were already in place: smog, a large population, and the danger of earthquakes!

The city's official birthday is September 4, 1781, the date of its founding by Spanish governor Felipe de Neve. The pueblo started out as what today we might call an "enterprise zone." If you agreed to make Los Angeles your new home, the government would provide you with an allowance of $116.50 a year, plus four horses, two cows, two goats, two sheep, one mule, and a yoke of oxen. And best of all, you wouldn't have to pay taxes for five years! In return for all this generosity, you were obligated to sell your surplus products, at prices fixed by the government, to the soldiers at the presidios in San Diego and Santa Barbara. You also were required to perform "community service," working to maintain the pueblo's streets and roads and public buildings.

In spite of--or perhaps because of--these arrangements, few settlers were willing to come. Only eleven families were on hand for the official founding of the pueblo in 1781. These "founding families" were a remarkably diverse group. Of the forty-six original settlers of Los Angeles, as many as twenty-six were of partial African ancestry.

The new pueblo was named after one of the many titles of the Virgin Mary, "our Lady, the Queen of the Angels." The name also included a local river, the Porciúncula, meaning ironically "little portion." The original name of the town was so long that some abbreviation was inevitable. So it was that over the years *El Pueblo de Nuestra Señora la Reina de los Angeles del Río de Porciúncula* became also known as L.A.

Something More ... Visit El Pueblo de Los Angeles State Historic Park, located in downtown Los Angeles across from the Union Railroad Station, 845 N. Alameda Street, Los Angeles 90012. Free. Tours available 10:00 A.M. to 1:00 P.M., Tuesday through Saturday. Telephone (213) 628-7164. Guided tours offered of twenty-seven historic buildings and sites of Los Angeles. An idealized bronze statue in the center of the plaza commemorates the founding of the pueblo.

LUCKY LINDY

I've always thought that the plane Charles Lindbergh flew across the Atlantic should have been named the *Spirit of San Diego* instead of the *Spirit of St. Louis*. After all, it was built in the Golden State, not the Show Me State.

"Lucky Lindy" was an immensely popular hero in the 1920s, a man whose courage and determination inspired tremendous admiration around the world. It was early in the Age of Flight when a New York City hotel owner put up $25,000 as a prize for the first aviator to fly non-stop from New York to Paris. Lindy's attempt began on the morning of May 20, 1927, when he took off from New York's Roosevelt Field a few minutes before eight o'clock. Thirty-three hours later, he touched down at Le Bourget Field just outside Paris. He was met by thousands of Parisians who came to celebrate the triumph of this slender, winsome Yank, the first aviator ever to fly solo from the United States to Europe. He was lifted off his feet by the throng of well wishers and carried prone above their heads. Losing sight of his plane, Lindy grimaced as he heard the ripping of fabric and the snapping of wood as hungry souvenir-hunters moved in. A couple of French pilots rescued him and drove him to the American embassy, stopping along the way to visit the *Arc de Triomphe* and the *Champs Elysses*. When Lindy at last bedded down at the embassy, having borrowed the ambassador's toothbrush and pajamas, he'd been awake for sixty-three hours.

Lindy's great adventure had begun three months earlier when he came to California and hired Ryan Aviation of San Diego to build him a plane. Claude Ryan and Charles Lindbergh had much in common. Both came from the Midwest, loved flying, and started their careers as barnstormers. Lindy's main concern was to make his new plane as light as possible to

maximize its range. This meant there would be no radio, no fuel gauges, and even the pilot's seat had to be a wicker chair. Lindy watched the work like a hawk. When one of Ryan's mechanics dropped a wrench and chipped a tiny piece of metal--about the size of a fingernail--from one of the engine's cooling fins, Lindy insisted on a whole new engine. At first the mechanic thought he must be kidding. When he realized the pilot was serious, the mechanic asked why he was being such a perfectionist. "I have my reasons," Lindy replied with a lopsided grin. "One is I'm a poor swimmer!"

Something More ... *Read the full story in Walter Ross, The Last Hero (1968). The California connection is told in Theodore Fuller, San Diego Originals (1987). The Spirit of St. Louis is on display at the Smithsonian Institution's National Air and Space Museum, located at the corner of Seventh and Independence avenues, Washington, D.C. 20560. Free. Telephone (202) 357-2700. Hours are 10:00 A.M. to 6:30 P.M. daily.*

EBENEZER AND THE *OTTER*

There's a special excitement watching ships come into a California port from some distant land. Flags from around the world snap in the breeze as these mighty vessels slowly make their way into the Los Angeles-Long Beach harbor or one of the many ports in San Francisco Bay.

The first American ship ever to reach California dropped anchor in Monterey Bay on October 29, 1796. Its captain, a crusty old salt named Ebenezer Dorr, came to California from Boston to hunt sea otter. The sea otter trade in the late eighteenth century was an immensely lucrative business. Those furry little marine mammals flourished in what were thought to be inexhaustible numbers from Baja California to the Aleutian Islands. The pelt of a fully-grown otter was about five feet long and two feet wide, with thick, black, glossy fur highlighted by silvery hair. Its value when shipped to the Chinese port of

Canton was about $300. Ebenezer Dorr collected hundreds of pelts along the coast and packed them on board his ship, aptly named the *Otter*. He then put in to Monterey for some fresh supplies.

California in 1796 was a remote outpost of the Spanish empire, governed by Spanish officials charged with guarding against foreign encroachment. The empire of Spain, like most European empires, was a closed system and foreign trade was discouraged or positively prohibited. California Governor Diego de Borica allowed Ebenezer Dorr to restock his ship with water and wood but specifically prohibited him from unloading any cargo or passengers. Captain Dorr, like many other Yankee visitors who would come to California in later years, was annoyed by these restrictions.

The *Otter* had on board some eleven passengers in addition to its twenty-six-man crew. The passengers were English convicts who had boarded while the ship was in Botany Bay, Australia. The arrangements Captain Dorr made with his passengers are not altogether clear, but most likely he'd agreed to take them to Boston for a price. Now he was having second thoughts. Despite the express prohibition of the Spanish governor, and over the vigorous protests of his passengers, old Ebenezer forced the convicts from the ship at gunpoint. Under the cover of darkness, he landed them on the beach at Carmel, stranding them there to an uncertain fate. What a guy! I've always thought that Ebenezer Dorr could hardly have been more heartless if his name had been Ebenezer Scrooge.

Something More ... Visit the old Custom House, a unit of the Monterey State Historical Monument, located at Custom House Plaza, Monterey 93940. Free. Open 10:00 A.M. to 4:00 P.M. November through February, and 10:00 A.M. to 5:00 P.M. March through October. Adele Ogden, The California Sea Otter Trade *(1941) tells the story of Ebenezer Dorr and his colleagues in this lucrative enterprise.*

FABULOUS FRESNO

When I read recently that those hip California Raisins had been enshrined in the Smithsonian's National Museum of American History, I was reminded of the history of Fresno, one of the premier cities in the state's bountiful heartland.

The town of Fresno was founded in 1872 when the Central Pacific Railroad extended its line through the San Joaquin Valley. The coming of the railroad opened up the vast agricultural potential of the valley and soon the land was dotted with fields and orchards. The dollar value of Fresno County's farm products today is greater than that of any other county in the nation. Among its leading crops are cotton, alfalfa, cantaloupes, plums, peaches, tomatoes, and lima beans. Fresno also proudly bears the title "Raisin Capital of the World." It produces annually about 60 percent of the world's raisins and some 90 percent of the raisins sold on the U.S. market.

The founder of the Fresno raisin industry was a fascinating fellow named M. Theo Kearney. His admirers called him "The Prince of Fresno" while his critics denounced him as the "Raisin Boss." He lived on a 5,000-acre estate in Fresno and in a luxury suite at the Palace Hotel in San Francisco. A life-long bachelor, Kearney enjoyed the company of beautiful women, including actress Lillie Langtry. When he died in 1906, he left an unusual provision for any future claimants to his fortune. His will provided fifty dollars for any person found to be his wife, and fifty dollars "to each and every person who in like manner" was found to be his child.

Although Theodore Kearney had no children, many native sons and daughters of Fresno have gone on to great fame and fortune. Playwright William Saroyan, a man who modestly billed himself as "the world's greatest writer," was born in Fresno in 1908 of Armenian immigrant parents. Another local progeny

is Fresno Junior College. Founded in 1910, it's the oldest junior college in California and one of the very first in the nation. Baseball great Tom Seaver was also born and raised in Fresno. He went on to become an All-American pitcher at the University of Southern California, and a three-time Cy Young award winner with the New York Mets. Then there are those beguiling California Raisins recently honored at the Smithsonian. The next time you see them strut their stuff to that funky beat of "I Heard it through the Grapevine," remember that they too are natives of fabulous Fresno.

Something More ... Visit the Kearney Mansion Museum, run by the Fresno City and County Historical Society. This masterpiece of Victorian domestic architecture is located at 7160 West Kearney Boulevard, Fresno 93706. Hours are 1:00 P.M. to 4:00 P.M., Friday through Sunday. Admission is adults $3.00 and children $1.00. Telephone (209) 441-0862. Also visit the Fresno Metropolitan Museum, 1555 Van Ness Avenue between Calaveras and Stanislaus streets, Fresno 93721. Hours are 11:00 A.M. to 7:00 P.M. Wednesday through Sunday. Admission is adults $2.00 and children and seniors, $1.00. Telephone (209) 441-1444.

IS THIS TRIP NECESSARY?

World War II was a time of tremendous sacrifice for all Americans. Tens of thousands of men and women in uniform gave their lives in defense of their country, while civilians on the home front also did their part to help the war effort. Civilian travel was discouraged so that vital resources could be reserved for the military. Signs in buses and railway cars sternly asked: "Is This Trip Necessary?" The question had special meaning for one group of Californians, the Japanese Americans.

On February 19, 1942, President Franklin Roosevelt signed Executive Order 9066, authorizing the removal of all Japanese Americans from their homes to what were called "relocation centers." This extraordinary act was justified at the time on grounds of military necessity. It's sobering to recall today that not one act of disloyalty--either of espionage or sabotage--was ever committed by any of the more than 112,000 Japanese Americans then living on the West Coast. While the Japanese Americans cooperated fully with relocation, many of them surely must have wondered, "Is This Trip Necessary?"

The Japanese Americans were placed first in temporary "assembly centers" at race tracks like Santa Anita in Arcadia and Tanforan in San Bruno. Then, during the summer of 1942, they were bussed to permanent relocation centers, two of which were in California. One was at Tule Lake in Modoc County near the Oregon border, and the other was at Manzanar in the Owens Valley of Inyo County. There they lived for the duration of the war in wooden barracks surrounded by barbed wire fences.

One of the best first-hand accounts of relocation is Jeanne Wakatsuki's haunting memoir of her girlhood at Manzanar. Through her young eyes, we see this desolate place as a typical American town in many ways. It had scout troops, sock hops, and baton-twirling lessons; but watching over it all were guard towers, searchlights, and machine guns. Men who never before had time for hobbies managed to create beautiful flower and rock gardens between the rows of barracks. School children had their own yearbook, but alongside every senior's picture was the name of the school he or she would have graduated from, outside the camp. Jeanne's brother sang with a forties dance band at Manzanar. Naturally they wanted to be an up-to-date American band, so they played all the top hits. By some strange coincidence, one of the most requested tunes was Cole Porter's "Don't Fence Me In."

Something More ... *Visit the site of the Manzanar War Relocation Center in the Owens Valley. The state historic marker at the gate reads: "May the injustices and humiliation suffered here...never emerge again." See also the collection of artifacts from the camp at the nearby Eastern California Museum, 155 Grant Street at Center Street, Independence 93526. Hours are 10:00 A.M. to 4:00 P.M. Free. Telephone (619) 878-2411. Read the full story in Jeanne Wakatsuki Houston and James D. Houston,* Farewell to Manzanar *(1973).*

WHEN THE SWALLOWS COME BACK TO CAPISTRANO

According to popular legend, it all began when an innkeeper near Mission San Juan Capistrano became annoyed at the hundreds of cliff swallows nesting on his property. He got so angry at the trespassers that he knocked down their nests and drove them all away. One of the mission padres happened to be standing nearby and took pity on these homeless birds. He called out, "Come, swallows, come to the mission. We will give you shelter. There is room enough for all." The displaced birds accepted his kind invitation and built their nests at the mission, where now they return each year on Saint Joseph's Day, March 19.

Actually the swallows arrive at San Juan Capistrano throughout the month of March. They've been sighted as early as March 3 and as late as March 22. Local boosters conveniently call the early arrivals "scouts" and those who come later "stragglers." Ornithologists are unsure how the swallows manage to calculate when to return. Apparently the birds have some sort of internal clock, in tune with the changing seasons. They begin their annual migration in Argentina and fly northward for 7,000 miles in about seven weeks.

After arriving at San Juan Capistrano, the swallows start building their nests with daubs of mud carried in their mouths. (There may be some partisanship here, for these mud-slinging birds are also called "Republican Swallows.") They build their nests in the arches high in the mission ruins. To get enough mud for their nests, they need open, muddy areas with plenty of puddles. The birds land in a puddle, roll the mud into a ball, and then fly away to their nests. Unfortunately, the rapid pace of development in this lovely part of southern California has reduced the available mud for the swallows. The number of returning and nesting swallows dwindles each year.

The swallows' arrival is always a time of great celebration in San Juan Capistrano. The town holds a week-long Swallows Festival that has included, among other attractions, a Toddlers' Marathon and an Ugliest Pet Contest. The priests at the old mission offer a special Mass of thanksgiving on Saint Joseph's Day and ring the 200-year old cast-iron bells. Thousands of tourists gather on that wondrous day, with binoculars at the ready, straining to see the incoming flock. Many expect to see the sky filled with swallows, all arriving like clockwork at precisely the same moment. Skeptics can do little to dampen the enthusiasm of the faithful. Some folks, after all, will swallow anything!

Something More ... Visit Mission San Juan Capistrano, 31882 Camino Capistrano at the corner of Ortega Highway, San Juan Capistrano 92675. Admission is adults $4 and children $3. Hours are 8:30 A.M. to 5:00 P.M. daily. Telephone (714) 248-2048.

KIPLING THE KIBITZER

Rudyard Kipling, author of such beloved classics as *Wee Willie Winkie* (1889) and *The Jungle Book* (1894), once paid a rare visit to California during a trip to the United States from his native India. Already well known as a writer and phrase-maker, Kipling was the inventor of such familiar expressions as "the white man's burden" and "fuzzy wuzzy."

During his visit in 1889, Rudyard Kipling freely expressed a great many unflattering opinions about the land and people he observed. "I love not the Americans in bulk," he readily confessed, and found their language to be particularly unpleasant. "They spit," he complained, "and their speech is not sweet to listen to." (Kipling wasn't very fuzzy about his American cousins, wuz he?) He also found Americans hopelessly unsophisticated. When he signed in at San Francisco's Palace Hotel

and listed his place of residence as India, an onlooker inquired, "And what did you think of Indiana when you came through?" He was appalled by the dining habits of the typical American. "Indeed he has no meals," Kipling concluded. "He stuffs for ten minutes thrice a day." He also professed to be outraged by the spectacle of public drunkenness and violent crime in America. He witnessed one Californian being stabbed in the eye and saw another shot at a poker game.

There were a few things about California that Rudyard Kipling found to his liking. He admired the strength of character and the generosity of spirit of the typical native-born Californian who is "devoid of fear, carries himself like a man, and has a heart as big as his boots." The landscape also evoked expressions of delight: "California's pine woods have a scent of their own, a sharp biting reek drawn out by the sun that sets the blood in motion and fills the idle mind with thoughts of going away into the woods and never coming back this side of eternity." He reserved his greatest praise for California's air and sunshine. "The climate of California," he said, "deals kindly with excess and treacherously covers up its traces. A man neither bloats nor shrivels in this dry air. He continues with a false bloom of health upon his cheeks...till a day of reckoning arrives."

Kipling gave the city of San Francisco a mixed review. He called its cable cars "contraptions of the devil," but thought its "large-boned, deep-chested, delicate-handed" women were angels. "San Francisco is a mad city," he concluded, "a city inhabited for the most part by perfectly insane people whose women are of remarkable beauty."

Something More ... Read Rudyard Kipling's letters, articles, and stories about his sojourn in the Golden State. They have been collected, edited, and thoroughly annotated by Thomas Pinney in Kipling in California *(1989).*

THE BAD MEN OF BODIE

The next time you find yourself travelling along the eastern side of the Sierra Nevada, and you have a little time to kill, consider visiting the old ghost town of Bodie. It's a quiet little place today, lovingly preserved in "arrested decay" as a state historic park. As you walk its deserted streets, imagine what it was like during its heyday when Bodie was known as one of the wildest, rip-roarin'est towns in the West.

The town of Bodie was founded after gold was discovered nearby in 1859 by a prospector named W. S. Bodey. Unfortunately, Bodey didn't live long enough to enjoy the riches of his claim. One winter's day he and his partner, a fellow named Taylor, got caught in a blinding snowstorm. When Bodey collapsed, Taylor tried to carry him on his back but finally had to abandon him in the snow, wrapping him in a heavy blanket. Taylor made his way back to their cabin, built a fire, and then went looking for his partner. The snow had covered everything. Taylor spent the rest of the winter alone in the cabin, haunted by what he imagined was Bodey's pitiful voice calling for help. When spring came and the snow melted, Taylor at last found his partner's remains...but the coyotes had gotten there first. All Taylor found were Bodey's bowie knife, revolver, blanket, and some clean-picked bones.

The mining town that grew up around Bodey's claim flourished in the 1860s and '70s. Its population of ten thousand was made up almost entirely of young men, about half of whom were foreign-born. Along Main Street were some fifty saloons, and only two churches--a typical ratio but one that boded ill for the town of Bodie. Legend has it that one murder occurred on the streets of Bodie every twenty-four hours. According to a popular story of the day, one little girl, told by her parents that they were moving to this God-forsaken town, knelt at her bedside and prayed, "Goodbye God, I'm going to Bodie."

The "Bad Men of Bodie" were known far and wide for their lawlessness. One of the most infamous of this notorious breed was Maneater Mike McGowan. He terrorized the townsfolk of Bodie by chomping on the sheriff's leg, threatening to chew off a judge's ears, and even attacking and eating a stray bulldog. He was arrested and charged with vagrancy, having "no visible means of support." One local newspaper thought there must be some mistake. "Mike has a visible means of support," the editor said. "He has an upper and a lower row of teeth!"

Something More ... Visit Bodie State Historic Park in Mono County during the spring or summer and explore its more than 168 buildings standing in various degrees of preservation. The only residents of the town are the park rangers and their families; there are no restaurants, overnight facilities, or service stations in this authentic California ghost town. To reach Bodie, take Highway 395 south from Bridge-port, and travel east on an unpaved road for thirteen miles. The story of Bodie's violent past is told in Roger McGrath, Gunfighters, Highwaymen & Vigilantes *(1984).*

CHARLEY'S BIG SECRET

Charley Parkhurst was a stagecoach driver in the 1850s and '60s, driving a four-horse team for Wells, Fargo and Company on the road from Santa Cruz to San Jose. Typical of the breed, Charley was known to take a nip at the roadhouses along the way and swear at the horses in a way that made the ladies blush. A companion later said that Charley "out-swore, out-drank, and out-chewed even the Monterey whalers." Charley was a tough-looking hombre with a patch over one eye, blinded by the kick of a horse. In later years, this colorful character was known as "Cock-eyed Charley."

I suppose it was Charley's skill as a driver that brought the greatest fame during the years when stagecoaches travelled the rugged terrain of the Santa Cruz mountains. After years of hard-driving and hard-living, Charley retired to a ranch near Twelve Mile House out of Santa Cruz and began raising stock.

When Charley died in 1879, the *San Francisco Morning Call* mourned the passing of "the most dexterous and celebrated of the California drivers, and it was an honor to occupy the spare end of the driver's seat when the fearless Charley Parkhurst held the reins of a four- or six-in-hand [four- or six-horse stage-coach]." It was only after Charley's death that the name "Charley Parkhurst" really became a legend, for only then was it revealed that there was more (or less) to Charley than what met the eye.

Charley Parkhurst, this extraordinary stage-coach driver who was taken to be a rough-and-tumble "good ol' boy," was, as a matter of fact, a woman. Before coming to California in 1851, from her native New England, Charley had even been a mother. She also was a voter, making her perhaps the first woman ever to cast a ballot in California!

Charley managed to disguise her secret identity over the years by wearing gloves (in both summer and winter) to hide her small hands, and wearing pleated shirts to hide her figure. These peculiar matters of dress were noted by contemporaries, but their significance was not understood. "He was thought to be putting on style," one journalist observed, "but as he always dressed well, the gloves were looked upon as a part of his high-toned ideas." Charley's high-pitched voice and beardless face had aroused some suspicion over the years, but even Charley's closest associates never knew. One family friend later recalled that Charley had always promised to tell him a "great secret." But somehow, Charley just never got around to it.

Something More ... Visit the grave of Charley Parkhurst in the Pioneer Cemetery, on Freedom Boulevard, Watsonville 95076. The entrance to the cemetery is at 66 Marin Street. Free. Telephone (408) 722-0310. Hours are 7:00 A.M. to 6:30 P.M. daily. ("Cock-eyed Charley" is not to be confused with another famous denizen of the Santa Cruz area, "Mountain Charley" McKiernan.) The story of Charley Parkhurst is briefly told in JoAnn Levy, They Saw the Elephant (1992).

THE CANALS OF VENICE

Abbot Kinney was about the closest thing to a "Renaissance man" California is ever likely to see. Heir to a cigarette fortune, he arrived in southern California in 1879 after travelling around the world. He settled near Pasadena and promptly became the champion of many worthy causes. He lobbied for the creation of national parks, served on a commission to investigate the condition of the California Indians, created almost single-handedly two local public libraries, founded the *Los Angeles Saturday Post*, and worked tirelessly promoting the virtues of the imported eucalyptus tree. Among his many publications was a curious little pamphlet on the rather intimate subject of *Tasks by Twilight* (1893).

The greatest enthusiasm of Abbot Kinney's later years was the planned community he called Venice. In 1904 he bought 160 acres of beach-front property about twenty-five miles from downtown Los Angeles. His plan was to create a development that combined both high culture and high profit. He built sixteen miles of concrete-lined canals, imported Venetian gondolas and gondoliers, and even constructed a scaled-down version of San Marcos Basilica. Along the canals, he built Renaissance-style homes that were intended to lure wealthy Californians who were "aesthetically inclined." As further inducements for the right sort of people, Kinney offered a full program of public education and entertainment. The high point of Venetian culture (California style) was a production of *Camille*, starring Sarah Bernhardt, performed at the end of an ocean pier.

Venice attracted many new residents, but they weren't all the well-heeled, high-minded types that developer Kinney had envisioned. By the early twentieth century, Venice was just another seaside resort with the usual array of raunchy amusements. The canals became stagnant and polluted, and eventually half of them were filled in. The remaining canals were condemned in 1942 and closed to the public. Then, in the 1950s, Venice evolved into a mecca for the beat generation, rivaling Greenwich Village in New York and San Francisco's North Beach. In the following decade, the old seaside town became the home of a new generation of free-thinking and free-loving Californians.

Today Venice is making something of a comeback. Its canals are registered as a national historic monument and six million dollars is being spent on a major restoration project. About three miles of the original canals are being refurbished, including a mile-long stretch of the Grand Canal. Many fine homes are being built, perhaps attracting at last the kind of folks that Abbot Kinney originally had hoped would come and live along his romantic canals. Now that the gondolas and gondoliers are returning, the strains of "O Solo Mio" and "Santa Lucia" may soon be wafting once again over California's very own canals of Venice.

Something More ... Visit the canals of Venice 90291. From the corner of Twenty-eighth and Dell avenues, stroll down Dell towards Venice Boulevard where you will cross over a series of four canals. One of the best books on the subject is John Arthur Maynard, Venice West *(1991).*

HAWAIIAN ROYALS

Natives of the Hawaiian Islands first arrived in California in the early 1800s. The islanders, then known as Kanakas, worked on ships engaged in the hide and tallow trade and in the hunting of sea otter. Richard Henry Dana offers a striking portrait of the Kanaka sailors of California in *Two Years Before the Mast* (1840).

During the gold rush, hundreds of Hawaiians came to California to work in the mines. Place names like Kanaka Creek in Sierra County and Trinity County's Kanaka Bar remind us of their early presence in the gold country. Two young members of the Hawaiian royal family even became 49ers, Prince Lot and Prince Alexander. Like boys everywhere, they weren't very conscientious about writing letters to the folks back home. Fifteen-year-old Prince Alexander later explained that he hadn't written because he didn't think his family and friends would "like to hear about sufferings and murder and gamblers."

Hawaii's Queen Emma arrived in San Francisco in 1866, receiving a twenty-one-gun salute from Fort Point as her ship sailed through the Golden Gate. She was the first queen ever to visit California and she charmed her hosts with her modest and unassuming ways. When she was introduced by one flustered San Franciscan as "Queen Victoria," she covered his embarrassment with a hearty laugh. King Kalakaua, known as "the Merry Monarch," visited California a few years later. The king was a great party-giver and party-goer. When he visited Chinatown, he enjoyed what was described as "the costliest Chinese dinner ever held in the United States." The menu included the traditional bird's nest soup, white snow fingers, imperial fish brains, shark fins, preserved eggs, turtle stew, and pear wine. The king returned to the city in 1891, staying at the Palace Hotel, and on that visit gained the dubious distinction of being the only king ever to die in California.

The last of the Hawaiian royals to visit California was Queen Liliuokalani in 1903. She arrived five years after Hawaii had been annexed by the United States. The former queen, frail and in ill health, was hardly noticed by the San Francisco press. But her niece, Princess Kaiulani, took the city by storm. Eighteen-year-old Princess Kai was glamorous, articulate, and decidedly cosmopolitan. As one local reporter put it, "Her clothes said Paris, her accent said London. Her figure said New York. Her heart said Hawaii."

Something More ... Read the marvelous account by John E. Baur, "When Royalty Came to California," in California History: The Magazine of the California Historical Society *(December 1988).*

A CALIFORNIA WEDDING

Planning a wedding by today's standards can really be a challenge, especially if you want something a little out of the ordinary. Looking for ideas? Consider the wedding customs of Old California, back in the days when this beautiful land was still a part of Mexico. The brides then, of course, were a bit younger than today. Girls in Old California usually were engaged at ten or twelve years of age, and wed between thirteen and sixteen.

Wedding festivities among the elite *Californio* families lasted from three days to a week or more, and for each event the bride wore a different outfit. To her wedding breakfast, she might wear a dress of brightly colored silk or satin; then change into a low-cut, short-sleeved gown of delicate pink or blue for the afternoon activities. For the actual wedding itself, the bride wore black. Her gown was often of silk brocade, with silk stockings and satin slippers. She wore her hair piled high on her head, accented by a beautiful tortoise-shell comb set with precious stones, and highlighted by an elegant black Spanish lace mantilla.

During the wedding ceremony, the bridegroom would present the priest with a roll of gold coins and two gold rings. After the padre blessed the rings, he would place them on the hands of the happy couple. The gold coins were placed on a tray which the bride, by custom, spilled to the floor. The coins thus became the property of the church.

Afterwards everyone repaired to the home of the father of the bride for a grand fiesta. The most common entertainment was a game called *casacarónes*, or the "egg frolic." Wedding guests would crack eggshells--filled with perfume, gold dust, or confetti--over each other's heads. When the eggs ran out, the guests sometimes moved on to slapping each other with wet napkins, or throwing pitchers and even buckets full of water. The partying really got out of hand at the de la Guerra wedding in Santa Barbara, where two giddy padres began slapping napkins and slinging buckets around, drenching everybody in the process. When the water ran out, one of the padres--apparently a real party animal--rushed into the bedroom, reached under the bed, grabbed the chamber pot, and flung its unpleasant contents in the face of an unsuspecting guest. Yuck! Well, perhaps that's *one* custom from Old California that today's brides and bridegrooms may wish to avoid after all!

Something More ... Read the classic accounts of weddings in Old California in Richard Henry Dana's Two Years before the Mast *(1840) and Alfred Robinson's* Life in California *(1846). See also Norine Dresser's highly entertaining article, "Marriage Customs in Early California," in* The Californians *(November/December 1991).*

OUR ITALY

Ever since the days of the gold rush, visitors to California have found that the landscape and climate of the Golden State reminded them of Italy. The similarities were so numerous that some even began calling California "Our Italy." The canyons of the Coast Range were reminiscent of the deep ravines of the Apennines, and the emerald-blue bays of Santa Catalina reminded travellers of the Isle of Capri. One visitor to the Russian River area in Sonoma County thought that he positively must be in Italy, perhaps somewhere along the Po River in Lombardy. "While visiting here," he said, "I veritably passed my time in Italy, for everyone I met and everything I saw, was Italian."

Italian immigrants came to California during the gold rush, but relatively few were miners. Instead, they found their "gold" in agriculture, fishing, banking, and retail trade. The center of the Italian community in San Francisco was North Beach, home of the city's fishing fleet. One of the early Italian settlers was a confectioner named Dominico Ghirardelli who made his fortune in chocolate. His factory today lives on as Ghirardelli Square, a hub-bub of shops and restaurants popular with tourists and residents alike. Another familiar name is that of Amadeo Peter Giannini, born in San Jose of Italian immigrant parents. In 1904 he opened a little bank in San Francisco which he called the Bank of Italy. Giannini later expanded his bank just a tad and rechristened it the Bank of America.

The Martini, Mondavi, and Petri families played key roles in the development of California's premium wine industry, while others enriched the state's culinary fare. America's oldest Italian restaurant, the Fior d'Italia, opened in San Francisco in 1886. The Marianetti brothers--Alfredo, Armido, Zefferio, and Giuseppe--offered such tempting entrees as veal sauté and calf brains for five cents a serving, and a complete steak dinner with all the trimmings for ninety-five cents. The Fior d'Italia was destroyed in the 1906 earthquake and fire, but was soon back in business serving minestrone--and nothing but minestrone--for about a month.

One of the most colorful of California's Italian immigrants was a banker from Genoa named Andrea Sbarbaro, founder of the Italian-Swiss Colony Winery at Asti. Inspired perhaps by the Villa d'Este in Rome, Andrea outfitted his villa in Asti with beautiful sparkling fountains. He was also quite the practical joker. After inviting his guests to settle into hammocks or seat themselves at sumptuous banquet tables on the lawn, Andrea Sbarbaro took great delight in turning on hidden sprinklers and giving all his guests an impromptu shower! *Sorpresa!*

Something More ... Visit the historic Ristorante Fior d'Italia, 601 Union Street, San Francisco 94133. Telephone (415) 986-1886 for reservations. A penetrating analysis of the "Italian metaphor" for California appears in Kevin Starr's landmark study, Americans and the California Dream *(1973). See also Deanna Gumina*, The Italians of San Francisco *(1978) and Andrew Rolle*, The Immigrant Upraised *(1968).*

AMELIA DID IT!

Amelia Earhart is one of the greatest aviators in American history, a woman whose many accomplishments too often have been overshadowed by the mystery of her disappearance somewhere over the South Pacific. Born in Kansas in 1897, Amelia Earhart was a highly intelligent and independent-minded young woman. She attended Columbia University and the University of Southern California in Los Angeles, but defied her parents' wishes by dropping out of college to earn money for flying lessons. Little did they know their daughter would someday make aviation history!

In 1928 Amelia Earhart became the first woman ever to make a transatlantic flight, just a year after Charles Lindbergh's famous flight from New York to Paris. Four years later she earned the nickname "Lady Lindy" by becoming the first woman to fly across the Atlantic solo, another milestone in the history of aviation. In 1935 she made the first solo flight (by anyone, male or female) from Hawaii to California. Ten pilots had already died trying to make that difficult crossing, and many observers feared that Amelia would be the eleventh. She took off from a soggy Wheeler Field in Honolulu and reached the California coast about twenty miles south of the Golden Gate. When she touched down in Oakland, her total flight time was more than eighteen hours. In a scene reminiscent of the pandemonium that greeted Lindbergh when he landed at Le Bourget Field outside Paris, ten thousand well-wishers were on hand in Oakland to greet Amelia Earhart.

Her last attempt to set a record was in 1937, when she took off to fly around the world. This was the fateful flight from which she never returned. To this day, no one knows for sure what happened to her but there have been plenty of theories. Some say that her navigator had been drinking the night before and was probably too hung over to have kept them

on course. Others speculate that her plane was downed by Japanese soldiers who thought she was an American spy. A couple of years ago an aluminum map case was found on a tiny Polynesian coral island, a tantalizing clue to what may have happened on that final flight.

Surely the great love of Amelia Earhart's life was flying. If she were around today, she'd probably have one of those "I'd Rather Be Flying" bumper-stickers on her car. But I'm not so sure about her husband George. During her first solo flight from Hawaii to California, he was asked by a reporter how he was holding up under all the stress. George gave the reporter an exhausted look and blurted out: "I'd rather be having a baby!"

Something More ... Visit the site of Amelia Earhart's enthusiastic reception at Oakland International Airport, 1 Airport Drive at Doolittle, Oakland 94621. Telephone (510) 577-4000. A plaque commemorating the event is located near the entrance to the main terminal. The mystery of her disappearance is recounted in Fred Goerner, The Search for Amelia Earhart *(1966).*

SQUIBOB

One of the most outrageous humorists in all the West was a young army officer named George Derby. He wrote under the pen name "Squibob" (pronounced SKWEE-bob), a word of his own invention that meant "there you go, with your eye out."

Lieutenant George Derby once wrote to his boss, Secretary of War Jefferson Davis, and suggested a few "modest proposals" for redesigning the regulation army uniform. He recommended adding a three-inch metal ring to the seat of the pants of every American soldier. It could be used by the cavalry to attach riders to their saddles, and by the infantry to retrieve foot soldiers who were retreating instead of advancing. He also had some recommendations for improving the officers' dress uniforms. Rather than gold braid epaulets, he suggested

something more practical: detachable hairbrushes. And oranges, he thought, would be far more useful on an officer's dress hat than the standard-issue pompons. Ol' Jeff Davis was not amused.

Lieutenant Derby was stationed in California in the early 1850s and soon had the state in an uproar. He upset some of the good citizens of Sonoma when he got the bright idea of switching a couple of babies in their buggies when their mothers weren't looking. A great joke, he thought, but the young lieutenant's wit was hardly appreciated by the babies or their mothers. Some of his other escapades were more benign and even humane. When a couple of his friends were determined to fight a duel, George made some phony bullets out of wax and colored them with charcoal--an early-day form of paint pellets, I suppose.

In San Diego, George Derby stirred up quite a fuss when a friend asked him to sit in as editor for a few days at the *Herald*. During the editor's absence, George pepped things up a bit by publishing fictitious news items and bogus illustrations. He also switched the political support of the paper from one party to another, and then described in advance the fight he expected when the editor returned. "We held him down over the press by our nose," George wrote, "which we had inserted between his teeth for that purpose."

George Derby truly became a legend in his own time for a joke he once played on his new bride and his dear old mother. Just prior to introducing them for the very first time, he solemnly confided to each that the other was practically stone deaf. Then he sat back, poker faced, and watched the shouting match begin!

Something More ... Read the Squibob *Papers (1856), a posthumously published collection of stories and sketches by George Derby. Also read George Stewart's biography,* John Phoenix, Esq.: The Veritable Squibob *(1937).*

THE STING
OF THE *BEE*

Did you know California's great Central Valley is filled with a passel of Bees? There's the *Fresno Bee*, the *Modesto Bee*, and the queen of them all, the *Sacramento Bee*. The first of the swarm was born in the capital city in 1857. Its unusual name was chosen for a couple of reasons. The paper's founders wanted a name that would stand out, and there certainly weren't any other papers around named the *Bee*. They also intended to work diligently to make their paper a success, and that hairy little honey-maker was the very epitome of industriousness, as in "busy as a bee."

The *Sacramento Bee* really came into its own under the leadership of a talented and feisty Irish immigrant named James McClatchy. He arrived in New York in 1841 and came to California during the gold rush, having quite an adventure along the way. He rode a mule some 1,500 miles to Mazatlan, Mexico, and from there he travelled aboard a ship whose captain was hopelessly incompetent. Apparently the captain sailed some 300 miles north along the *wrong* side of the Baja Peninsula, and then had to sail back to Mazatlan before coming north again to California. (Too bad there wasn't a "frequent sailor" program in those days!)

More adventures awaited James McClatchy in the Golden State. He was arrested and jailed in 1850 for his outspoken views on behalf of the "squatters" who settled Sacramento. A riot broke out when his friends and supporters tried to spring him from the riverboat jail tied up along the city's waterfront. He eventually was released and went on to fight for the things he believed in as editor of what became the city's leading newspaper.

After James McClatchy died in 1883, his son C. K. McClatchy took over as editor of the *Bee* and continued the hard-hitting editorial policies that his father had begun. C.K. once criticized the state legislature by running a headline at the end of the 1893 session, "Thank God the Session Now is Almost Over!" The leaders of the legislature took offense and threatened to move their entire operation back to the state's first capital, San Jose. C.K. regarded this as a thinly veiled attempt at censorship. He ran a political cartoon the next day showing a relocated capitol in San Jose with a scaffold outside and a hangman's noose reserved for the first reporter who writes: "Thank God, the Legislature has Adjourned." The cartoon also added a gratuitous insult to the fine city of San Jose by showing the new capitol surrounded by such low-life enterprises as a pool hall, gambling den, wine room, dog pit, and a massage parlor. Once again, the *Bee* had stung!

Something More ... View the excellent display of early Sacramento journalism, including a complete print shop, in the McClatchy Collection of the Sacramento History Museum, 101 I Street, Sacramento 95814. Admission is adults $3.00 and children $1.50. Hours are 10:00 A.M. to 4:30 P.M., Wednesday through Sunday. Telephone (916) 264-7057. Enjoy the outrageous humor and stinging barbs in Don Stanley and Frank McCulloch, (eds.), The Sting of the Bee (1982).

ISADORA THE FREE

The sculptor Rodin called her "the greatest woman the world has ever known." She was talented, she was beautiful, and she was free. Her name was Isadora Duncan.

Born near San Francisco's Union Square in 1877, Isadora grew up in "genteel poverty" in an extremely unconventional home. Her father was a ne'er-do-well who abandoned his wife and children, leaving them destitute. The Duncans moved to Oakland and lived for a time near the girlhood home of the poet Gertrude Stein. When the two later met in Paris, Isadora confessed that as a girl she had often swiped apples from the Stein's Oakland orchard.

Isadora Duncan was just ten years old when she dropped out of school (what she called her "prison") and began giving dancing lessons to neighborhood children. This was the beginning of her lifelong passion for the dance. She and her mother moved to New York when she was eighteen and later travelled by cattle ship to London. Neither regretted leaving the Bay Area. "We must leave this place," Isadora said, "for we shall never be able to accomplish anything here." After arriving in Europe, Isadora danced in public parks and on the stage in Paris and Moscow. She created her own Temple of the Dance in Athens for performances of her uniquely romantic style. Her sensual, free-flowing movements, according to one critic, "awakened a frenzy of enthusiasm" from the men in her audience.

This remarkable woman rebelled against convention in both her professional and private life. She rejected anything she considered unnatural and tried always to imitate in her dance the natural rhythms of the body--running, skipping, and walking. She performed in her bare feet, wearing long, flowing white gowns held in place by a golden cord. She's known, even today, as the woman who "freed the dance." She denounced marriage as an unnecessary restraint on the freedom of women, and had affairs with (among others) a tango dancer, a Russian poet, a boxer, a San Francisco music critic, and a stoker on a ship. She bore three children, each of whom had a different father. She once summed up her all-embracing philosophy of life like this: "All men are my brothers, all women are my sisters, and all little children on earth are my children." One defender of more traditional values responded with an acid tongue, "Evidently all men are her brothers, for not one is her husband."

Something More ... Visit the birthplace of Isadora Duncan at 501 Taylor Street, San Francisco 94102. A plaque marks the spot between Post and Geary. If you're in a reading mood, you might check out her autobiography, My Life *(1927), or if you'd rather watch a video, rent* Isadora *(1969), starring Vanessa Redgrave in the title role.*

THE PITS

Long before southern California was crisscrossed by freeways growling with traffic, it was the home of saber-tooth cats, shaggy camels, giant vultures, huge mastodons, and woolly mammoths. They lived in an environment quite different from ours today, for California's climate then was more humid and its vegetation more lush. One of the best ways to visualize this ancient time is to visit the La Brea tar pits in Los Angeles' Hancock Park.

The pits were formed thousands of years ago as oil was forced to the surface by heat and movement of the earth's crust. As the lighter petroleum elements evaporated, a mass of sticky black asphalt was left behind. This asphalt was a valuable resource for the Indians of the Los Angeles basin. They used it as a bonding agent and to waterproof their baskets. Early settlers from Mexico used the tar (*la brea,* in Spanish) to cover their roofs and to seal their boats. In the later 1800s, American entrepreneurs took asphalt from the pits and sold it as fuel. Serious scientific investigation of the site began in the early 1900s and has continued ever since. The most spectacular find so far has been the remains of an imperial mammoth standing thirteen feet high and weighing over 20,000 pounds. Its ivory tusks curl outward and upward for more than ten feet. Only one human skeleton has been found in the pits. Paleontologists in 1914 discovered the remains of someone they promptly dubbed "La Brea Woman." She stood about four feet ten inches tall, and lived in the Los Angeles area 9,000 years ago. The total number of bones taken from the pits now numbers over half a million, representing more than 4,000 mammals and an equal number of birds.

How did so many animals end up in the pits? Winter rains often covered the surface of the tar with pools of water, thus attracting unsuspecting animals. Imagine this scene 20,000

years ago: A California camel comes galumphing by and stops for a drink. He wanders down to the edge of a likely-looking pond, but soon finds his hooves stuck in the thick tar beneath the surface. He struggles in vain to break free. His cries of frustration attract a prowling saber-tooth cat who moves in for the kill. The two animals flail about in the water and soon the tiger is stuck too. A pair of vultures circles overhead and lands for a quick meal. Their wings get encrusted with tar and they too find themselves trapped. Soon they all sink below the surface, predators and victims alike, caught in the deadly grip of this sticky mass. These poor critters only wanted a drink and a bite to eat. To end up like this, man, was really the pits!

Something More ... Visit the La Brea pits and the adjoining George C. Page Museum, 5801 Wilshire Boulevard, Los Angeles 90036. Hours are 10 A.M. to 5 P.M., Tuesday through Sunday. Admission is $5.00 for adults and $2.50 for students and senior citizens. Telephone (213) 936-2230 for a 24-hour recorded message or (213) 857-6311 during museum hours. A good read on the pits is Chester Stock, Rancho La Brea (1930).

CODE TALKERS

Over 240,000 Native Americans live in California today, many of whom are descendants of the first people who settled this land thousands of years ago. Also included in the Native American population are more recent arrivals, people who came to California from reservations all across the United States.

During the early days of World War II, a very special group of Native Americans arrived in the Golden State. They came from the great Navajo reservation in Arizona, New Mexico, and Utah, and were assigned to a top-secret Communication School Training Center near San Diego. There they developed a secret code for use on the battlefields overseas. The code included over 400 Navajo words for the most frequently used terms in the military lexicon. The Navajo word for "buzzard" became the code name for a bomber, an "owl" was an observation plane, and a "chicken hawk" was a dive bomber. Battleships were known by the Navajo word for "whale," submarines were "iron fish," and destroyers were "sharks." The Navajo also had special names for the enemy, words that weren't officially a part of the code. They called Mussolini "Big Gourd Chin," and Hitler was known as "Mustache Smeller." Each letter of the alphabet also received a Navajo name so that words not in the code could be spelled out. The letter A was the Navajo word for "ant," B was "bear," all the way through "yucca" for Y and "zinc" for Z. The code was so effective that even Navajos who did not know the code were unable to decipher it.

Eventually 450 Navajos served as "code talkers" in the United States Marines on battlefields throughout the Central and South Pacific. When necessary, the code talkers fought alongside their fellow Leathernecks and risked their lives as troubleshooters and stretcher-bearers. Their service was absolutely essential in several key engagements. "Were it not for the Navajos," commented one officer, "the Marines would never have taken Iwo Jima!"

The folks back home at the training center in California were mighty proud of the code talkers. At the war's end, the *San Diego Union* tried to sum up the Navajo's contribution (and may have inadvertently maligned their beautifully complex language in the process): "Huddled over their radio sets in bobbing assault barges, in foxholes on the beach, in slit trenches deep in the jungle, the Navajo Marines transmitted and received messages.... For three years, wherever the Marines landed, the [enemy] got an earful of strange gurgling noises interspersed with other sounds resembling the call of a Tibetan monk and the sound of a hot water bottle being emptied."

Something More ... Read the comprehensive account of The Navajo Code Talkers *(1973) by Doris A. Paul. The definitive study of the wartime experiences of Native Americans is Alison R. Bernstein,* American Indians and World War II *(1991).*

WOMEN AND THE BAR

When was the last time you described your lawyer as having "exquisitely turned deep red lips, dimpled cheeks, a broad, firm chin and a complexion without rival"? That's the way one admirer described Clara Shortridge Foltz, the first woman ever admitted to the bar in California.

Clara grew up as an Iowa farm girl and eloped at the tender age of fifteen to marry a handsome Union soldier named Jeremiah Foltz. The young couple came out to San Jose, California, in the mid-1870s, and it was there that Clara decided she wanted to be a lawyer. But she soon found that no law school would admit her. Nor would the state of California allow her to take the bar exam...all on account of her sex.

When Hastings Law School in San Francisco refused to admit Clara Foltz in 1879, she decided to take legal action.

The school's attorney argued that to admit women would "interfere with the proper discipline and instruction of the students." The attorney complimented the "grace and beauty" of the young applicant, but argued that "lady lawyers were dangerous to justice inasmuch as an impartial jury would be impossible when a lovely lady pleaded the case of the criminal." Clara Foltz rejected these arguments as groundless. The court agreed and ordered Hastings to admit all qualified applicants regardless of sex.

Clara Foltz thus enrolled in law school, but her fellow students didn't exactly welcome her with open arms. As she later recalled, "If I turned over a page in my notebook, every student in the class did likewise. If I moved my chair--hitch went every chair in the room."

Before she could become a lawyer, Clara Foltz also needed to pass the state bar exam. But California state law at the time limited the practice of law to "white males only." So Clara drafted legislation to eliminate both gender and racial discrimination in the legal profession, and she fought successfully to get her bill passed by the legislature. Opposing lawmakers condemned the bill and issued dire warnings that women would be "un-sexed by practicing law." Clara Foltz responded in kind, using some remarkably "gender-specific" language of her own to denounce her opponents. "Narrow gauge statesmen grew as red as turkey gobblers," she said, "mouthing their ignorance against the bill, and staid old grangers who had never seen the inside of a courthouse seemed to have been given the gift of tongues and then delivered themselves of maiden speeches pregnant with eloquent nonsense."

Something More ... Read the forthcoming biography of Clara Foltz by Stanford Law Professor Barbara Allen Babcock. Professor Babcock has already published several articles on this courageous legal pioneer in the Arizona Law Review *(1988), the* Indiana Law Review *(1991), and the* Cincinnati Law Review *(1992).*

THE FRANCIS DRAKE MYSTERIES

The English sea dog Francis Drake sailed from England in December of 1577 as a privateer, commissioned by Queen Elizabeth I to raid Spanish shipping and settlements in the Americas. For a year and a half, Drake had a field day loading some thirty tons of Spanish gold and silver aboard his ship the *Golden Hind*. But his greed nearly did him in. By the time he reached the California coast in June of 1579, his ship was literally bursting at the seams with its ill-gotten Spanish booty. Drake was forced to put in to shore and make emergency repairs.

The exact location of Drake's landing spot, at what he called "New Albion," remains a mystery. Some historians vote for San Francisco Bay while others say he landed at Bolinas Lagoon. Most scholars agree that he probably put in at Drake's Bay on the Point Reyes Peninsula in Marin County. One of the most convincing bits of evidence that points to Drake's Bay is the description made by the English visitors of the local Indians who greeted them by crying and scratching their cheeks. The English interpreted this response (rather presumptuously, I've always thought) as an act of worship and concluded that the natives believed them to be gods. We now know that this was a mourning custom of the Coast Miwok people of Marin. Apparently the Indians believed these Englishmen were all dead men--ghosts--because they were so pasty white!

Another of the great Francis Drake mysteries is the "plate of brass" left behind to claim the land for Queen Elizabeth. In 1936 a young man said he found such a plate near Point San Quentin in Marin County. He delivered it to the University of California, Berkeley, where Professor Herbert Eugene Bolton declared it to be authentic and proudly put it on display at the Bancroft Library. Forty years later, however, new scientific tests

at the Lawrence Berkeley Laboratory and at Oxford University revealed that the plate was most likely a fake. Analysis of the metal corresponded to brass of the twentieth century rather than the sixteenth, and x-ray tests revealed that the brass was produced by a modern rolling process unknown at the time of Drake.

So what are the true origins of that plate of brass? For years Professor Bolton had told the students in his history classes "to keep an eye out for Drake's plate." Perhaps some conniving students got together and produced the plate as a hoax on their poor old history professor!

Something More ... View the "plate of brass" on display at the Bancroft Library, University of California, Berkeley 94720. Open Monday through Friday, 9:00 am to 5:00 pm, and Saturday, 1:00 pm to 5:00 pm. Free admission. Telephone (510) 642-6481. The most thorough account of the controversies surrounding Francis Drake is Warren Hanna, Lost Harbour *(1979).*

BREAKING UP IS HARD TO DO

Once again a proposal is making the rounds to divide California. It's an idea that's been around since the days of the gold rush. At first, it was the folks of southern California who wanted to separate from the rest of the state because they thought they were paying more than their fair share of the state's taxes. In 1859, Los Angeles Assemblyman Andrés Pico introduced a bill to split the state along the northern border of San Luis Obispo, Kern, and San Bernardino counties. The plan was approved by the state legislature but rejected by Congress. Many members of Congress were convinced that this split-state movement, coming on the eve of the Civil War, was somehow a pro-Southern conspiracy. They didn't realize it was actually an early-day version of the California taxpayers' revolt!

The idea came back with a vengeance in the early 1960s. This time it was the northern Californians who wanted to secede, and the divisive issue was reapportionment. The Supreme Court had recently mandated a new plan for apportioning the state senate, giving southern California control just as it had already gained control of the assembly. When the plan went into effect, many northern Californians decided it was high time to declare their independence. Several northern senators proposed a split at the Tehachapis. One senator from Santa Rosa even asked whether a proposal for armed insurrection would be in order!

Water played a key role in triggering the movement again in the late 1970s. The proposed building of the Peripheral Canal, which would have doubled the flow of water from the north to the south, led one Bay Area assemblyman to warn: "Please, southerners, don't think you can rob our water and destroy our ecosystem, because there will be a civil war in this state if you do."

The most recent proposal to split the state came once again from the citizens of the far northern counties. Some favored creating the fifty-first state of Northern California and renaming the rest of the state Southern California. One assemblyman from Shasta County even introduced legislation in the early 1990s to divide California into *three* new states. As proof that people were taking the split-state movement seriously, the assemblyman noted that the game show "Jeopardy" recently added a new category called the fifty-first state. This was, indeed, an ominous sign. With the movement to divide the state being discussed in Jeopardese, who can deny that the great California mitosis is near at hand? Stay tuned.

Something More ... Read all about the long-standing rivalry between northern and southern California in Michael DiLeo's fascinating account, Two Californias: The Truth about the Split-State Movement *(1983).*

A SUNNY FIELD AND PEA SOUP

One of the most unusual towns in all of California was founded in 1911 by a group of Danish professors and ministers from Iowa. They bought some 10,000 acres in Santa Barbara County's beautiful Santa Ynez Valley, staked out their town, and named it Solvang, which in Danish means "sunny field."

Over the years, Solvang has worked hard to retain much of its original Danish flavor. Some families still practice the quaint customs of the old country. *Fastelavn* is held each year in the spring, on the day before the beginning of Lent. According to tradition, all the parents are allowed to sleep in on this special day while the children rise early. (That part sounds pretty good. Mom and Dad can lounge around in bed, drinking coffee and enjoying a Danish or two.) When the kids think the time is just right, they come into their parents' room with fancy switches and give them both a spanking. Ouch!

Tourism is far-and-away the major industry in Solvang today. More than three million tourists come to town each year, visiting the shops and enjoying the scrumptious Danish pastries. The aromas drifting out of the bakeries are really spectacular. A friend of mine insists that Solvang is the only town where you can gain weight just walking down the sidewalk. The biggest attraction is Danish Days, held each summer since 1936. Townsfolk dress up in native Danish costumes, the men in tasseled caps and knee breeches and the ladies decked out in bonnets and brightly-colored shawls. There's usually some excellent theater at night, including dramatic presentations of stories from everybody's favorite great Dane, Hans Christian Andersen.

Just three miles west of Solvang is Buellton, "The Home of Split Pea Soup." This all began about sixty years ago when a

local innkeeper added to his menu some split-pea soup, based on a recipe from his French mother-in-law. The soup was such a big hit that other establishments in town began serving pea soup too, each claiming to be the home of the authentic and original creation. Two restaurants on one side of Main Street posted huge signs which said "The Home of Pea Soup" and "The Best Split-Pea Soup in the World." Meanwhile, across the street, another enterprising restauranteur put up an even bigger sign that proudly proclaimed: "We are the Originators of the Split-pea soup advertised across the Street."

Something More ... Visit the Elverhoy Museum, 1624 Elverhoy Way, Solvang 93464. Open from 1:00 P.M. to 4:00 P.M., Wednesday through Sunday. Tours are by appointment. Telephone (805) 686-1211. Also be sure and visit "Hap-Pea" and "Pea-Wee" at Pea Soup Andersen's, 376 Avenue of the Flags, Buellton 93427. Telephone (805) 688-5581.

BULLS AND BEARS

Long before California was the home of the Warriors and the Angels, the Giants and the Rams, it was a place where the bulls and the bears were a big part of the sporting scene.

During the annual rodeos of Mexican California, mounted *vaqueros* (later known as buckaroos or cowboys) would "cut out" and brand the stock. They often reserved the largest and most ferocious of the bulls for the bull ring; there these hapless bovines would confront local matadors on foot or on horseback. In San Francisco, the community bull ring was at the foot of Russian Hill, near what is today the intersection of Columbus and Vallejo streets.

The favorite sporting event in Old California was what were called "bull and bear fights." Fearless *vaqueros* would capture a grizzly, take him to the bull ring, and tie or chain his

hindfoot to the forefoot of one of those enormous, long-horned California bulls. Folks would then place their bets, sit back, and wait for the swatting, goring, and biting to begin. Whoever survived the fight was declared the winner. This was no place for the faint of heart! Indeed, the following play-by-play account should be read only if you've got a sound heart *and* a strong stomach.

Forewarned, gentle reader, read on. "The bull began the fight by charging the grizzly with his horns. A blow from the grizzly's paw did not stop the onset. In a moment they were rolling over each other in the dust. But the bear finally, though badly gored, got his teeth fastened into the bull's neck, and the bull was pulled to his knees." (Watch out, here's where things really get ugly!) "The bull's tongue hung out. This was what the bear wanted. He got his claw into the bull's mouth, pulled the tongue out still further, and then bit it off. With this the bull gave up the contest, and soon after both animals were dispatched."

There may be some connection between such bloody contests and the terms used to describe the ups and downs of the nation's stock market today. Some scholars believe that the bulls and bears of Wall Street came from England, but others claim that it was Horace Greeley, the editor of the *New York Tribune*, who first coined the terms "a bull market" and "a bear market." We know that editor Greeley was in California in the 1850s and that he witnessed one of these terrifying fights between a bull and a bear. When he got back to New York, he applied the terms to the nation's stock market. So the next time you read about the bulls and the bears on the financial page of your morning newspaper, remember that those contentious beasts may have started out here, long ago, on the sports page of Old California.

Something More... Read more about bull and bear fights, and other sporting events, in Richard L. Sandwick, "Bloody Sundays," in Davis and Judy Dutton (eds.), Tales of Monterey *(1974).*

ABE LINCOLN'S CALIFORNIA DREAM

SURF'S UP!

You may have noticed that California seems to hold a special appeal for presidents and former presidents alike. Several recent chief executives have enjoyed vacationing in California, and both Herbert Hoover and Ronald Reagan spent their golden years in the Golden State. But did you know that Abraham Lincoln also had a deep and abiding interest in California?

Our sixteenth president often enjoyed visiting with Californians who came to Washington. Among his guests at the White House were Noah Brooks, a reporter for the *Sacramento Union*, and Mariano Guadalupe Vallejo, the great *Californio* leader from Sonoma. One of Lincoln's closest friends was Edward Baker, a long-time California resident for whom San Francisco's Fort Baker is named. Baker had been one of Lincoln's early political rivals in Illinois, having defeated Lincoln in his bid for Congress in 1844. Later the two became such close friends and political allies that the future president named his second son Edward Baker Lincoln. In 1852 Baker moved to California and became a successful attorney and public speaker. He helped swing California behind Lincoln in the presidential election of 1860. Then, early in the Civil War, Baker was killed while leading his union regiment in the battle of Balls Bluff near Leesburg, Virginia. Lincoln was deeply grieved by the loss of his friend and wanted very much to come to San Francisco someday and visit his grave.

Abe Lincoln never made it to California -- the bullet of John Wilkes Booth made that impossible. Early on the day he was assassinated, Lincoln met with two California-bound visitors, Congressman Cornelius Cole and Speaker of the House Schuyler Colfax. Both men soon were leaving for California, and Lincoln engaged them in a long and animated conversation about their trip. The president suggested that California would be a wonderful place for demobilizing the troops after the war. He said he intended to "point them to the gold and silver waiting in the West." The president's last officially recorded conversation was with Colfax, and it ended with the words, "A pleasant journey to you.... I'll telegraph you in San Francisco."

Shortly before Lincoln left for Ford's Theater on that fateful day, April 14, 1865, the president and his wife went for a buggy ride and discussed their plans for the future. She told him she'd like to take a trip to Europe, but he insisted he'd rather go to California and see the gold mines and the redwoods. Lincoln even dreamed of retiring in California. He thought it would be a perfect place to raise their two sons. In a line that could have been spoken by Ronald Reagan more than a century later, Abraham Lincoln said wistfully that he thought the California climate made the Golden State just the right place for "Father and Mother to spend their old age."

Something More ... Visit the grave of Edward Baker, just as Abraham Lincoln hoped someday to do. It's located in the San Francisco National Cemetery, at the Presidio, near the intersection of Lincoln and Sheridan streets, San Francisco 94129. Free. Open daylight hours daily. Telephone (415) 561-2008. Read the full story in Milton Shute's informative book, Lincoln and California *(1943).*

THE ALLENSWORTH STORY

We're all familiar today with the important role African Americans have played in our nation's armed forces. Popular films such as *Glory* and *A Soldier's Story* remind us of the long and sometimes painful history of blacks in the military.

Allen Allensworth was an African American soldier who served with distinction in the United States Army. He was born a slave in Kentucky in 1842, and somehow managed to master the illegal arts (for slaves) of reading and writing. During the Civil War he escaped from slavery and joined the Union army. After the war he left the military, enrolled in college, attended a theological seminary, and became a minister. He later re-enlisted and was appointed chaplain of the all-black 24th Infantry, one of the units known proudly as "the Buffalo Soldiers." Following an injury in the Philippines during the Spanish-American War, he returned to the states and served as a chaplain on Angel Island in San Francisco Bay. When he retired as a lieutenant colonel in 1906, Allen Allensworth was the highest ranking black officer in American history.

After leaving the army, Col. Allensworth and his family settled in Los Angeles. It was there that he came up with the idea of establishing a self-sufficient, all-black California town, a place where African Americans could live their lives free of the racial discrimination that so often plagued them elsewhere. His dream was to build a town where black people might live and create "sentiment favorable to intellectual and industrial liberty." In 1908 he founded the Tulare County town of Allensworth, a new settlement in the heart of the San Joaquin Valley about thirty miles north of Bakersfield. The black settlers of Allensworth built homes, laid out streets, and put up public buildings. They organized a glee club, an orchestra, a brass band, and a Women's Improvement Club. Soon there was a

church, a school, and a thriving blacksmith shop, livery stable, barber shop, and drug store.

But the town soon ran into some serious problems. The dry and dusty soil made farming difficult, and poisons seeped into the drinking water. When a state legislator proposed building an industrial school in Allensworth, African Americans in Los Angeles opposed the proposal. They feared that this experiment in black self-sufficiency was really a step backwards toward racial segregation and would lead to further division in American society.

The town lost its founding father in 1914 when Col. Allensworth was killed in an automobile accident in Los Angeles. The town's discouraged settlers drifted away in the next couple of decades and Allensworth was reduced almost to a ghost town...its streets paved, someone said, with broken dreams.

Something More ... Visit Colonel Allensworth State Historic Park. The park is easily accessible from State Route 43, about eight miles west of Earlimart on State Route 99. Open 8:00 A.M. to 4:30 P.M. daily. Admission is $3.00 per car. Telephone (805) 849-3433. The story of Allensworth is included in Kenneth Hamilton, Black Towns and Profit *(1991).*

CLAMPERS

Some Californians are Elks, others are Moose, and some even are Lions. But the most colorful of them all are the Clampers, members of the Ancient and Honorable Order of E Clampus Vitus, a fraternal organization founded back in the gold rush days. Apparently it all began as a spoof on other lodges and secret societies, but its history is a little difficult to reconstruct. The early meetings of E Clampus Vitus were devoted so completely to drinking and carousing that none of the Clampers was ever in any condition to keep minutes, let alone remember what had happened the next day!

The Clampers claimed that all their members were officers and "of equal indignity," but some, such as the Clampatriarch and the Noble Grand Humbug, were more equal than others. The official purpose of the Order was to take care of the widows and orphans...especially the widows.

According to tradition, a person could join E Clampus Vitus by invitation only and then was expected to endure an elaborate and grueling initiation ceremony. Sometimes he was blindfolded and seated on a cold wet sponge in the bottom of a wheelbarrow. One of the brothers would take him for a ride "on the rocky road to Dublin" over the rungs of a ladder laid on the floor. Or the recruit might be asked if he believed in "the Elevation of Man," and if he answered yes, he'd be lifted high into the air by a block and tackle. Once a Clamper had survived his own harrowing initiation, he was powerfully motivated to get even by putting some other new recruit through the same rigmarole.

Membership in E Clampus Vitus declined in the late 1800s, but experienced a revival in the 1930s and is still going strong today. Modern-day Clampers typically dress up in gold-rush garb--usually a red miner's shirt, black hat, and Levi's-- and they still hold outrageous initiation ceremonies. They specialize now in putting up commemorative plaques at places like saloons, bawdy houses, and other sites that may have been overlooked by more serious historical societies. Lots of folks don't know what to make of the Clampers today, but I think Carl Wheat, one of the founders of the revived Order back in the thirties, put it well when he described E Clampus Vitus as "the comic strip on the page of California history."

Something More ... Visit the Calaveras County town of Murphys, the "unofficial capital of all Clamperdom." See the Old Timers Museum in the Peter L. Traver Building, and the Wall of Comparative Ovations of E Clampus Vitus which is a display of more than seventy Clamper plaques commemorating colorful personalities and incidents in California history, located on the outside of the Thompson Building. Both buildings are side by side at the corner of Main Street and Sheep Ranch Road, Murphys 95247. The best history of the organization is Lois Rather, Men Will Be Boys *(1980).*

A RUBE GOLDBERG DEVICE

Not many of us achieve sufficient fame or notoriety that our name ends up in everyday language. We call a traitor a "Benedict Arnold" and sign our "John Hancock" on the dotted line, but few other examples come to mind. Perhaps the only Californian to be so honored was a native San Franciscan named Rube Goldberg.

Reuben Lucius Goldberg was born on the fourth of July in 1883, graduated from San Francisco's Lowell High School, and received his engineering degree from the University of California, Berkeley. His first job was designing sewer lines and water mains for the city of San Francisco, but he soon lost interest in so mundane a calling. He'd always enjoyed doodling and drawing sketches for his friends, so in 1904 he got a job as a sports cartoonist with the *San Francisco Chronicle*. He then moved on to New York where he developed several syndicated cartoon features, including "Mike & Ike--They Look Alike," "Lala Palooza," and "Boob McNutt." He started on a modest scale, making just thirty dollars a week, but eventually his features were pulling in an amazing 1.5 million dollars a year. For Rube Goldberg, drawing cartoons proved to be a lot more fun--and a lot more profitable--than designing sewer lines!

Rube Goldberg's most successful cartoon was a series called "Inventions," starring the inimitable Professor Lucifer Gorgonzola Butts. The good professor's contraptions usually included a fantastically complex set of pulleys and ropes as well as odd bits like bees buzzing, dogs wagging their tails, or moths devouring socks. Each step in the process was neatly labelled with a running commentary of instructions off to the side. The feature enjoyed enormous popularity because Goldberg tapped into his readers' frustration with all the needless complications of modern life, something we can certainly relate to today as we struggle with our VCRs, cellular phones, and fax machines. Much of the technological wizardry with which we have surrounded ourselves fits well the dictionary's definition of a Rube Goldberg device: "any contrivance that achieves by extremely complex means what actually could be done simply."

In Rube Goldberg's later years, he switched from drawing comics to creating editorial cartoons. He won a Pulitzer Prize in 1948 for an ominous cartoon of a typical American home resting on an atomic bomb and tottering over a chasm labelled "World Destruction." Shortly before he died in 1970, Rube Goldberg offered a prophecy for the year 2070. His vision of the future may already have come true: "Politicians kissing babies and making promises, women demanding equal rights, and fathers misunderstood by their sons."

Something More ... Read Rube Goldberg's hilarious book How to Remove Cotton from a Bottle of Aspirin (1959). Other examples of his work can be found in Clark Kinnaird (ed.), Rube Goldberg vs. The Machine Age (1968) and Peter C. Marzio, Rube Goldberg (1973).

W. C. FIELDS FOREVER

"I'm free of all prejudices," W. C. Fields once boasted. "I hate everybody equally." So it was that one of America's most beloved comics endeared himself to countless fans across the country and around the world.

W. C. Fields was born William Claude Dukenfield in Philadelphia in 1879. He left home when he was eleven years old and tried at first to make a living as a juggler. By the time he turned twenty he was a star on the vaudeville stage, appearing with the likes of Will Rogers and Fanny Brice. He was also a radio personality, trading quips with that wooden-headed dummy, Charlie McCarthy.

Films such as *You Can't Cheat an Honest Man* (1939), *The Bank Dick* (1940), and *Never Give a Sucker an Even Break* (1941) were among his finest efforts. My all-time favorite, though, is *My Little Chickadee* (1940), co-starring the inimitable Mae West. W. C. Fields played essentially the same character in all his films, a slightly befuddled poop, always with a martini near at hand. His speech was peppered with his own peculiar brand of profanity. "Godfrey Daniel!" he would growl in mock agony, or explode in exasperation with "Great Mother of Pearl!" He invented a whole series of characters with names such as J. Frothingham Waterbury, Filthy McNasty, F. Snoopington Pinkerton, and Cuthbert J. Twillie.

Like the great Irish wit Oscar Wilde, W. C. Fields endowed the world with a splendid array of witticisms. "Women are like elephants," he once said. "I like to look at them but I wouldn't want to own one." His politics remained decently shrouded behind such cryptic remarks as "I never vote for anyone. I always vote against." And it's appropriate that the star of the film, *The Fatal Glass of Beer* (1933) should also have observed, "Somebody left the cork out of my lunch." One line often identified with this outlandish eccentric actually may have been spoken *about* him by a churlish friend: "Anyone who hates small dogs and children can't be all bad." I've always been especially fond of his fatherly advice to the over-achiever. "If at first you don't succeed, try again," he advised. "Then quit. No use being a damn fool about it."

W. C. Fields died in Pasadena on Christmas Day, 1946. Perhaps his best-remembered line is the epitaph he wrote for his own tombstone: "On the whole, I'd rather be in Philadelphia."

Something More ... Read the story of this comic genius in Ronald Fields' intimate biography, W. C. Fields *(1984), or bask in Martin Lewis' compilation of* The Quotations of W. C. Fields *(1976). Happily many of the films of W. C. Fields are now available on video.*

NO GIGGLING, PLEASE

The army's Fort Ord on the Monterey Peninsula bears the name of one Edward Otho Cresap Ord, a young soldier who came to California in 1847 during the Mexican War. Lieutenant Ord later worked his way up to the rank of major general, drafted the first city map of Los Angeles, and was appointed commander of the Department of the Pacific.

During his early days in California, Ord served alongside another young officer who went on to great fame during the Civil War, William Tecumseh Sherman. Both Ord and Sherman were intrigued by the land and people of California. One evening, in February of 1847, the two young lieutenants made an unexpected call on an old and rather stout *Californio* named José Gomez. They arrived just in time for dinner but Señor Gomez didn't relish the prospect of having to share his supper of stewed rabbit and tortillas with these two gringo officers. Begrudgingly he invited them to join him at his table. "Down we sat," Sherman later recalled, "and Lieutenant Ord and I helped ourselves to a dish of rabbit, with what I thought to be an abundant sauce of tomato. Taking a good mouthful, I felt as though I had taken liquid fire; the tomato was *chili colorado*, or red pepper, of the purest kind. It nearly killed me, and I saw Gomez's eyes twinkle for he saw that his share of the supper was thus increased. I contented myself with bits of meat and an abundant supply of tortillas. Ord was better case-hardened than I, and he stood it better."

The fort that bears the name of this "case-hardened" young officer served its country well from World War I to the end of the Cold War. The base was founded in 1917 when the federal government purchased some 15,000 acres of sand dunes and scrub oak on the Monterey Peninsula. By World War II it had doubled in size and become a major staging ground and training post for troops heading to the Pacific theater. Among the many soldiers who experienced the joys of basic training at Fort Ord was the future actor and mayor of the nearby town of Carmel, Clint Eastwood.

Fort Ord is scheduled for closure by 1997, part of the post-Cold War reduction of the nation's armed forces. As local residents mourn its passing, one part of the Fort Ord story bears repeating. Before the base took its current name, it was known as Gigling Reservation, named after a German family who once lived in the area. The base was soon rechristened. Apparently the brass didn't think that "Gigling" was an appropriate name for an army base--even if it was one "g" short!

Something More ... Read the full story of Lieutenant Ord and his many colleagues in the military conquest of California in Neal Harlow, California Conquered: War and Peace on the Pacific, 1846-1850 *(1982).*

THE AUSTRIAN CONNECTION

All through California's colorful history, people have come to the Golden State from lands around the world. Each group of newcomers has made its own unique contribution to the mosaic that is California culture. Among those who have come are the people of Austria. By 1870 more than a thousand Austrians were living in California, mining gold and planting orchards and vineyards. One enterprising colony of Austrians built a winery along the banks of Los Gatos Creek in Santa Clara County, at a place now known as Austrian Gulch. All was well until a cloudburst in 1889 washed away the winery's foundations and sent thousands of gallons of wine gushing into

the creek. It was a disaster for the Austrian vintners, but the folks downstream enjoyed a bonanza of *soupe de poisson* and *bouillabaisse*!

Some of the best-known Hollywood film personalities have come from Austria. Arnold Schwarzenegger, that hulking muscleman who starred in such blockbusters as *Conan the Barbarian* (1982) and *The Terminator* (1984), was born in 1947 in Graz, Austria. Film-maker Otto Preminger was born in Vienna in 1906. One of his biggest films was *Exodus* (1960), an epic which ran for nearly four hours. When Preminger gave a private screening for his friends, comedian Mort Sahl stood up after about three-and-a-half hours and complained loudly, "Otto, let my people go!" Scriptwriter Billy Wilder was also Austrian-born. His most successful films were *The Seven Year Itch* (1955) and *Some Like It Hot* (1959). Wilder was famous for his wit both on and off the screen. Once when he was in Paris, his wife in California asked him to bring home a bidet. After shopping around Paris unsuccessfully, Wilder telegraphed his wife: "Unable obtain bidet. Suggest handstand in shower."

Actress Hedy Lamarr was born Hedwig Kiesler in Vienna in 1913. She entered the film industry in 1929 and created quite a sensation when she appeared nude in the film *Ecstasy* (1933). Later one of her wealthy husbands was so taken by the film that he tried to buy up every print. Perhaps Hedy Lamarr's most famous film was *Samson and Delilah*, released in 1949, in which she starred with an early-day Conan named Victor Mature. One of the critics of the film, Groucho Marx, was a little disappointed by what he saw. "I didn't care much for *Samson and Delilah*," Groucho remarked. "No picture can hold my interest when the leading man's bust is bigger than the leading lady's."

Something More ... Rent some of the classic Hollywood films that illustrate the "Austrian connection" in California culture. A terrific reference book on the motion picture industry is Leslie Halliwell, Halliwell's Filmgoer's Companion *(1988).*

SEEING THE ELEPHANT

Louise Amelia Knapp Smith Clappe (phew!) came to California during the gold rush and lived for over a year in a rough-and-tumble mining camp along the Feather River. She's known to us today by a marvelous series of letters she published under the pen name "Dame Shirley."

The letters of Dame Shirley are a valuable resource because they provide a woman's perspective on life in the gold rush. They contain a wealth of detail on the interior furnishings of miners' cabins, the clothing worn by the forty-niners, and their typical daily fare. Her descriptions are so vivid that they were later used by other writers, including Bret Harte and Mark Twain. Two of Harte's best known stories, "The Luck of Roaring Camp" and "The Outcasts of Poker Flat," were based in part on incidents she had described. Even Mark Twain's most famous California yarn, "The Celebrated Jumping Frog of Calaveras County," may have been based on one of Dame

Shirley's letters. Hollywood has also used her letters. Lee Marvin and Clint Eastwood starred in *Paint Your Wagon* (1969), one of the many films based on details drawn from Dame Shirley.

The letters of Dame Shirley are also a lot of fun because they tell us about the miners' unusual language. She had an especially keen ear for their odd figures of speech. Perhaps the strangest phrase she heard was "about your clothes." If a miner wished to borrow something, he might inquire if you had it "about your clothes." Dame Shirley first heard this odd bit of "minerese" when she was asked one evening at dinner, "Excuse me, madam, do you have a pickle about your clothes?" Another unique expression was "seeing the elephant" which meant having a truly remarkable experience, something as unusual and unexpected as encountering in the mines an elephant...or a fine lady like Dame Shirley.

Dame Shirley later became a teacher in the San Francisco public schools, teaching for twenty-four years. She enjoyed taking her students on Saturday outings to the ocean along the city's western shore and telling stories about the early days of California. I like to think of her there on the beach at the close of the day, gathering her students around her. "I've got a few stories for you," she would begin. The students could see the sparkle in her eyes, even in the fading glow of twilight. They knew the stories she was about to tell were true, for these were stories about her own adventures in the California gold rush of long ago.

Something More ... Visit the Plumas County Museum, 500 Jackson Street, Quincy 95971. Free. Hours are 8:00 A.M. to 5:00 P.M. Monday through Friday year-round, and 10:00 A.M. to 4:00 P.M. on Saturday and Sunday during the summer. Telephone (916) 283-1750. Rent a video of the movie Paint Your Wagon *with Lee Marvin, Clint Eastwood, and Jean Seberg. (Clint even sings in it!) A recent book for young readers about this remarkable Californian is Jim Rawls,* Dame Shirley and the Gold Rush *(1993).*

LIMANTOUR SPIT

One of the finest places in northern California for a picnic on the beach is Limantour Spit, a long, narrow point of land at Drake's Bay in the Point Reyes National Seashore. Whenever I'm there, enjoying some cold cuts and a loaf of French bread, I'm reminded of the story of José Yves Limantour, a true scoundrel who once had all of San Francisco in a tizzy.

José Limantour was a native of France who came to California in 1841 when this land was governed by Mexico. He made a good living in the shipping trade, importing French silks, perfumes, and brandy to the culture-hungry citizens of Old California. One of his ships foundered and sank at Limantour Spit, thus the name for this lovely beach where now picnickers frolic among the dunes.

After California became a part of the United States in 1848, Limantour claimed that Mexican Governor Manuel Micheltorena had earlier granted him an enormous amount of land, totalling nearly a million acres. He said that all the property in San Francisco south of California Street was his--as well as Alcatraz, Yerba Buena, the Farallons, and parts of Marin, Napa, and Sonoma counties. Lots of other folks thought the land was theirs and they fought Limantour in court. When a federal lands commission ruled in Limantour's favor in 1856, he began selling off his lots at exorbitant prices. The people of San Francisco weren't about to take this lying down! They hired lawyers to snoop around and try to find out the low-down on this José Limantour. Two years later, in 1858, a federal judge reversed the lands commission ruling, declaring that Limantour's claims were based on perjured testimony, the signatures on his grants were forgeries, and the seals on his deeds were counterfeit.

Limantour was charged with fraud, arrested, and released from jail after posting a $30,000 bond. Then he disappeared, most likely fleeing across the border to Mexico, never to return. Few people today remember him at all, but for a time he was one of the most infamous characters in all of California. And so it is that José Yves Limantour--importer of French silks, real estate baron, and scoundrel extraordinaire--is all but forgotten today. All we have left of Limantour...is his Spit.

Something More ... Visit Limantour Spit for a picnic of your own, and don't forget the Grey Poupon. From Highway 1 at the town of Olema, turn west on Bear Valley Road into the Point Reyes National Seashore 94956. Just past the visitors center, turn left on Limantour Road which ends at the beach (about 8 miles). Free. Daylight hours only. Telephone (415) 663-1092. The best account of this colorful miscreant is Kenneth Johnson's biography, José Yves Limantour v. The United States *(1961).*

HOG WALLOWS OF CALIFORNIA

The next time you visit your favorite health spa for a soothing mud bath, you might take along your copy of *Dr. History's Sampler* and regale your fellow bathers with a little history lesson.

Wallows, you should explain, are places where animals roll about or lie in the dirt or mud for refreshment and (apparently) for their own amusement. Huge pits and mounds called "elephant wallows" dot the plains of Africa, and much of the San Joaquin Valley was once covered with what were called "hog wallows." These great mounds of earth were about fifty feet long, twenty feet wide, and around six feet high. Geologists think they were probably formed by gas and water escaping through cracks in the earth. Others say they were made by giant gophers! I prefer the account of the Yokuts Indians who believe these mysterious mounds were leftover work baskets used in the creation of the Sierra Nevada.

Unfortunately most of the hog wallows were leveled years ago by California farmers. At least one mound still remains, thanks to the Buckman family, who preserved ten wallowy acres in their natural state near Lindcove in the San Joaquin Valley. The Tulare County Historical Society has put a handsome marker there, pointing the way.

Even though these wallows weren't really made by hogs, swine have played an important role in California history. (How's that for a segue?) Pigs were first introduced by the Spanish padres, and later raised at Fort Ross by the Russians. The great California "pig boom," though, was during the gold rush. By the 1880s, the state's swine population had bulged to over half a million. One leading hog farmer was a fellow we've met before, Philip Danforth Armour, the gold-rush butcher who started his meat-packing career in Placerville. Author Jack London was another enthusiastic hog farmer; he built an elaborate "pig palace" on his ranch in Glen Ellen. California also has a large population of wild boar, first introduced in Monterey County in the 1920s for game hunting. More recently, some of these wild boar have been trained to do police work! They have a tremendous sense of smell and can sniff out odoriferous suspects from a quarter-mile away.

As for your garden-variety domestic California swine, you can see plenty of them, up close and personal, on pig farms throughout the state. There they are, cavorting in the mud, doing their best to keep alive that grand tradition of California hog wallowing. Soo-ee!

Something More ... Visit the hog wallows of Tulare County. The historical marker is on the northern edge of the preserve, located on Avenue 314 just west of Road 220, near Lindcove. See also the Tulare County Historical Society Museum, 27000 South Mooney Blvd., Visalia 93277. Hours are Thursday through Monday, 10:00 A.M. to 4:00 P.M. Telephone (209) 733-6616.

JEDEDIAH AND THE BEAVER

Crossing overland to California during the gold rush was incredibly difficult. The thousands who came followed trails blazed by those from the United States who had come before. The first to make that perilous crossing was a young man named Jedediah Strong Smith.

Jedediah's middle name suited him well. His courage was formidable and his character was as solid as a rock. He once was attacked by a grizzly bear that grabbed him around the head with its huge paw and ripped off part of his scalp and an ear. (Remember the story of the bull and bear fight? Maybe this rambunctious grizzly was trying to get at Jedediah's tongue!) Jedediah remained calm and somehow managed to escape. Later, without flinching, he had a companion sew his skin and ear back on with a needle and thread. In many ways, Jedediah was unlike the typical mountain man of the far west. Our popular image of this "reckless breed of men" is that they were a wild and woolly bunch. But Jedediah was a tidy and quiet man, tall and slender, with blue eyes and light brown hair. Even in the wilderness he shaved everyday...being careful, of course, not to dislodge his recently re-attached ear. He never used tobacco or profanity, and imbibed only occasionally of a little wine or brandy. Jedediah Smith was really an unlikely sort of western hero at a time when it was said that God took care to stay on his own side of the Missouri.

Jedediah Smith arrived in Mexican California in December of 1827, having crossed overland through the Mojave Desert, and was promptly arrested and ordered to leave the province. The Mexican authorities had never seen anybody like him before so they decided he must be an American spy. But Jedediah was no spy; he'd come to California to collect beaver pelts, not intelligence.

You might wonder how such a nice young man as this ever got into the beaver business in the first place. It all started when Jedediah was looking through the newspaper one day and saw a help-wanted ad for beaver trappers. The ad said there were jobs across the wide Missouri for one hundred enterprising young men who were willing to work steadily for the next two or three years. Jedediah answered the ad and was on his way to becoming one of the great beaver trappers of the West. Perhaps many of us today, faced with economic uncertainty, would also welcome such an ad. It offered job security, high adventure, and a chance to work in the great outdoors--all in pursuit of that furry little critter, the beaver.

Something More ... Visit the Jedediah Smith State Park near Crescent City 95531. It's a wonderful place to hike and camp, but no beaver trapping allowed! From Highway 101, travel east on Highway 199 to the park. Admission is $5.00 per vehicle. Telephone (707) 458-3310 for camping information and park hours. Dale Morgan's Jedediah Smith and the Opening of the West (1953) *is a brilliant biography.*

MUDVILLE

Future newspaper titan William Randolph Hearst first got into the publishing business while he was an undergraduate at Harvard University in the early 1880s. He was the business manager of the campus humor magazine, the *Harvard Lampoon*. Willie Hearst, as he was known in those days, also gained a well-deserved reputation for being a mischievous practical joker. It was said that Willie once sneaked a jackass, all brushed and groomed, into a profess or's room. When the prof returned, he found the ass with a card tied to a ribbon 'round its neck. The card read, "Now there are two of you!" Then there was the (probably apocryphal) prank that may have ended young Willie's days at Harvard. The legend is that he delivered to each of his professors a package. In each package was a chamber pot with the prof's name elaborately inscribed on the inside bottom!

After William Randolph Hearst left Harvard, his father gave him a "consolation prize," the editorship of the *San Francisco Examiner*. He soon assembled a fine staff of writers, including one of his old buddies from the *Harvard Lampoon*, a brilliant young philosophy major named Ernest Lawrence Thayer. Readers of the *Examiner* on June 3, 1888, turned to page four and read a poem by Thayer about a baseball team from Mudville. The poem, printed in the *Examiner* for the first time anywhere, told of a player, Casey by name, who was at the plate in the bottom of the ninth, with two men on and two men out. On the last pitch of the game, Casey gave a mighty swing...

> Oh! somewhere in this favored land the sun is shining bright;
> The band is playing somewhere, and somewhere hearts are light.
> And somewhere men are laughing, and somewhere children shout;
> But there is no joy in Mudville--Mighty Casey has struck out.

"Casey at the Bat" went on to become a revered bit of Americana, recited by generations of schoolchildren and cherished by lovers of the National Pastime. The poem's early fame can be attributed largely to a vaudeville actor named William de Wolf Hopper (future husband of columnist Hedda Hopper) who took the poem on tour. By his own count, Hopper recited the poem at least 15,000 times during his lifetime.

The lineage of "Casey" is thus a colorful one. Prankster Willie Hearst first published the poem and a vaudevillian made it famous. But it was a philosophy major who conceived Casey and brought him to life. Years later Ernest Lawrence Thayer was inducted into Baseball's Hall of Fame...most likely the only *magna cum laude* Harvard graduate ever to be so honored!

Something More ... Read all about the origins of this treasured verse in Ernest Thayer's own Casey at the Bat: A Centennial Edition *(1988). The story of Willie Hearst's years at Harvard appears in W. A. Swanberg,* Citizen Hearst *(1961) and Judith Robinson,* The Hearsts: An American Dynasty *(1991).*

FREE FOREVER

This is the story of Biddy Mason, one of California's most intrepid African American pioneers. Born a slave on a Georgia plantation in 1818, she was taken west by her owner in 1848, the year gold was discovered in California. Her owner's family of seven and Biddy's family of four settled first in Utah. Three years later they moved again, this time to San Bernardino, California. Biddy Mason made both moves, several thousand miles in all, on foot, herding livestock in the dust behind her owner's wagon.

California at the time was officially a free state. The constitution of 1849 was very clear about this: "Neither slavery nor involuntary servitude shall ever be tolerated in this state." Nevertheless thousands of slaves like Biddy Mason and her family were brought to California by their masters and kept in bondage. To make matters worse, state law prohibited blacks from testifying against whites in any California courtroom. This made it nearly impossible for slaves to take legal action to win their freedom. But Biddy Mason was one of the fortunate ones. When her owner attempted to take her back to the slave-holding south, a California attorney agreed to fight for her right to stay. The attorney then accepted a bribe to drop her case, but the judge learned of this wrongdoing and ruled in Biddy's favor, proclaiming that she and her family were "entitled to their freedom and are free forever."

Biddy Mason, free at last, stayed in California and went on to become one of the first African American women to own property in Los Angeles, very near what later became the heart of the city's financial district. From her home on Spring Street, Biddy tended her family, helped the poor, and founded the first African Methodist Episcopal Church, a church that's still going strong today. During her lifetime, Biddy was probably best known as a midwife, skilled in what was then called "catching babies." Today she's regarded as a founder of the professions of nursing and midwifery in Los Angeles and as one of the great early-day philanthropists in the African American community.

Biddy Mason lived and worked in Los Angeles until her death in 1891, and death alone stopped her from helping all those who came to her in need. She was a woman with a large and generous heart. "If you hold your hand closed," Biddy was fond of saying, "nothing good can come in. The open hand is blessed, for it gives in abundance, even as it receives."

Something More ... Visit the public art project in downtown Los Angeles, "Biddy Mason's Place--A Passage in Time," located on South Spring Street, between 3rd and 4th streets, next to the Bradbury Building, Los Angeles 90013. The project director, Dolores Hayden, is also the author of the article "Biddy Mason's Los Angeles, 1856-1891," in California History: The Magazine of the California Historical Society *(Fall 1989).*

BOONTLING

Attention parents! Do you sometimes have trouble understanding your children? Or how about you kids. Do you ever have a hard time understanding your parents? Of course you do! From time immemorial, communication between children and adults has been a challenge. But things really got out of hand about a century ago in Mendocino County, the home of "Boontling."

It all started as a game among the children of Boonville, a quiet little town in the Anderson Valley. The kids there wanted to talk among themselves without being understood by any pesky grown-ups. They began making up words and phrases to confound their elders and called their language "the Boont lingo," or "Boontling" for short. Kids have done this sort of thing for ages, in cultures around the world, but what makes Boontling so unusual is that it's survived for over a century now, passed on from one generation to the next.

MOLDUNES!

Credit for inventing this unique language is usually given to a couple of boys named Ed "Squirrel" Clement and his buddy Lank McGimsey. While out at their favorite swimming hole on the Navarro River in the summer of 1890, they started making up words. Soon other kids picked up the lingo. Then when school started in the fall, the teachers had to learn some Boontling in order to survive. Surprisingly, the older folks of Anderson Valley began using it as well. Boontling became a kind of badge of identity, distinguishing valley residents from outsiders. Over the years the language has grown to include more than a thousand different words and phrases.

Here's a typical bit of "Boont lingo." See if you can figure it out. "There're some kimmies japin broadies to the airtight." Does that make any sense? "Kimmies" comes from the Scots, meaning "men." "Japin" means "driving," based on a local stage driver named J. P. "Broadies" is a contraction derived from "broad-horned cattle," and "airtight" is the word for "sawmill." Put it all together and you've got, "There're some men driving cattle to the sawmill." What they were going to do with those poor cows at the sawmill, I have no idea.

Other examples of Boontling are "deejy" (not to be confused with "dee-jay") which is a contraction for "degenerate," "killing snakes" means "working very hard," "Moldunes" translates as "unusually large women," "Saul's grandmother" means "dead," and my very favorite bit of the Boont lingo is "pack-'em-out-billies," meaning "dirty socks." Speaking of which, the next time you're killing snakes make sure that your pack-'em-out-billies aren't japin your friends bonkers!

Something More ... Visit the Anderson Valley Historical Museum, located in the Little Red School House, three miles west of town, near the corner of Highway 128 and Anderson Valley Way, Boonville 95415. Free. Telephone (707) 895-3207. Winter hours are 1:00 P.M. to 4:00 P.M. Monday through Sunday, 11:00 A.M. to 4:00 P.M. in the summer. Also read Myrtle Rawles, Boontling, or the Strange Boonville Language *(1967).*

THE RISE AND FALL OF BRET HARTE

SHRIEK!

AUTOGRAPHS

California writer Bret Harte had the misfortune of being a man who peaked too soon. He enjoyed great success and fame early in life, but lived another thirty years in the shadow of his former glory.

Francis Brett Harte was born in Albany, New York, in 1836 and moved to California when his widowed mother married a man who later became the mayor of Oakland. His most productive years were spent in San Francisco where he wrote for the city's two leading literary magazines, the *Golden Era* and the grand old *Overland Monthly*. For a time, Bret was at the center of the city's cultural and social elite. He achieved his greatest fame with the publication of his tales of the gold rush era. Stories like "The Luck of Roaring Camp," "The

Outcasts of Poker Flat," and "M'liss" transformed the California gold rush into a grand myth for the West.

Unfortunately for Bret Harte, he was never able to match his youthful successes. Much of his later work was mediocre and the critics became increasingly harsh. In 1870 Bret left California never to return, announcing that he was heading back east to establish a "Society of Escaped Californians." Eventually he sailed to Europe and settled near London. His last years were spent grinding out variations of his old stories and poems for which the English seemed to have an insatiable appetite. At times he was reduced to selling his autograph to admirers. He secretly loathed those who sought a souvenir of his former greatness. "I cannot help saying how utterly heartless, soulless, indelicate, insincere, and vulgar [are] the whole tribe of autograph hungerers," he once confessed.

Bret Harte died in 1902 and lies buried in the little town of Frimley, about thirty miles southwest of London. His grave is marked with a simple red granite stone. It's a very moving experience to visit this site and think about how far this enormously talented writer had travelled from his youth in the California gold country. When a fellow Californian visited his grave some years ago, he placed there an evergreen bough and recalled the words Bret Harte had written upon the death of Charles Dickens:

> And on that grave where English oak and holly
>   And laurel wreathes entwine,
> Deem not all a too presumptuous folly--
>   This spray of Western pine.

Something More ... See the Bret Harte Plaque on the Post Street side of the Bohemian Club, 624 Taylor Street, San Francisco 94102. Harte's best works are collected in The Outcasts of Poker Flat and Other Tales *(1964). The grave of Bret Harte is described in Lawrence Powell,* California Classics: The Creative Literature of the Golden State *(1971).*

LOW-DOWN ON LODI

Who can resist the romantic spell cast by Tony Bennett's "I Left My Heart in San Francisco" or the mellow rhythms of Dionne Warwick's "Do You Know the Way to San Jose?" These upbeat celebrations, enjoyed by visitors and residents alike, have done a marvelous job of boosting two of northern California's most populous cities. Folks in the San Joaquin County town of Lodi have not been so fortunate. The song that once made their town a household word includes a memorable--and mournful--complaint about being "stuck in Lodi again."

The word "Lodi" surely has a lovely sound. It's origins, as with so much that is fascinating about California history, are uncertain. Most experts agree that the name commemorates the Battle of Lodi in Italy, one of the great battles of the Napoleonic Wars. Others claim the name was chosen because some of the town's early settlers came from Lodi, Illinois, and they wanted to name the place for the town back home. Still others say the name was selected to honor a fleet-footed filly who recently had won a race in Sacramento. An original oil painting of this possible namesake once hung in the reference room of the Lodi public library.

Like many communities in the Central Valley, Lodi is renowned for its production of fruits and vegetables. In the late 1800s it was the "Watermelon Capital of the World," producing such scrumptious varieties as the Black Diamond, Rattlesnake, and sweet Klickly melons. Tokay and Zinfandel grapes were introduced in the early 1900s, and for many years the crowing of Queen Zinfandel highlighted the annual Tokay Festival. The ceremonial arch at Pine and Sacramento streets was put up in 1907 to celebrate the festival of that year.

Now about that song that brought such illfame to this fair city. John Fogerty, the lead vocalist for Creedence Clearwater Revival, wrote the ballad back in 1969. It tells the story of the backroads odyssey of a down-and-out rock and roll band. Fogerty chose the name "Lodi" from a notebook of unusual words and phrases he'd put together as a kid growing up in Berkeley. He later said he intended no offense by the song and that he'd never even visited the town as a musician. Four years after the song was a big hit, John Fogerty and his family happened to be passing through Lodi on a fishing trip when their van nearly ran out of gas. As the engine began to sputter, he turned to his children in the back seat, smiled, and said, "Well kids...it looks like we're going be 'stuck in Lodi again!'"

Something More ... Listen to the song that made Lodi famous. It's on the Creedence Clearwater Revival album called Green River *(1969). Visit the Lodi Historical Museum, 11793 N. Micke Grove Road, Lodi 95240. Admission 50 cents for children 6 to 12 years and seniors, $1.00 for adults. Hours are 1:00 P.M. to 5:00 P.M. Wednesday through Sunday. Telephone (209) 368-9154. A wonderful overview of the history of Lodi is available in Naomi Carey,* Mountain Men to Astronauts *(1969).*

THE CALIFORNIA ADVENTURES
OF WYATT EARP

Most folks remember Wyatt Earp as the dapper United States Marshal who survived the shootout at the OK Corral in Tombstone, Arizona. But Wyatt Earp was also a Californian. He spent a dozen years in San Diego, moonlighting as a prize-fight referee and operating three downtown gambling halls. During twenty-five of his "golden years," he wintered in a cottage in the San Bernardino County community of Vidal, near the town that today bears his name, Earp, California.

Wyatt Berry Stapp Earp was born in Illinois in 1848, the same year that gold was discovered in California, and grew up on an Iowa farm. Wyatt and two of his brothers, Virgil and Morgan, were known as the "fighting Earps," and all three became sheriffs or marshals in some of the wildest cowtowns of the West, places like Wichita and Dodge City. After Wyatt's older brother Virgil moved to Arizona, Wyatt followed in 1879. He soon became a deputy sheriff and also rode shotgun for Wells, Fargo, and Company between Tombstone and Tucson. Wyatt then became the marshal in Tombstone, and it was there that he met his future wife Josephine, better known as Josie.

Josie Earp had left her home in San Francisco when she was just eighteen to join a company of itinerant actors. She was incredibly beautiful, with long black hair and intense, dark brown eyes. (She reminds me of Morticia of the Addams Family.) Thirteen years younger than Wyatt, Josie could be both charming and headstrong. One of Wyatt's friends found her somewhat intimidating. He said that the reason *he'd* never married was that he was afraid of winding up with a "shrew" like Josie.

Wyatt's and Josie's time together in California was stormy. Their fortunes rose and fell depending on Wyatt's gambling houses and real-estate investments. Both the Earps

also loved to play the horses; Wyatt won a fine trotting horse in a poker game and soon added more horses to his string. Josie later wrote a book about their life together and revealed some of the terrific battles she had with America's most famous peace officer. "When I got him mad," she wrote, "he would fill and light his pipe, put on his hat and walk out. Any wife who has had this happen knows *that* is the most exasperating thing a husband can do."

Something More ... Visit the graves of Wyatt and Josie Earp in the Hills of Eternity Memorial Park, 1301 El Camino Boulevard, Colma 94014. Hours are 8:00 A.M. to 4:30 P.M. Monday through Friday, and 8:30 to 2:30 on Sunday (closed Saturday). Wyatt died at the age of eighty-one on January 13, 1929; Josie lived on to the ripe old age of eighty-three. A biographical sketch of this fascinating pair appears in Theodore Fuller's highly entertaining collection of San Diego Originals *(1987). For the full story, see Josephine Earp,* I Married Wyatt Earp *(1976).*

A GIFT FOR SILVER STREET

The Birds' Christmas Carol (1887) by Kate Douglas Wiggin has warmed the hearts of millions of readers over the years. But few are aware that this holiday classic was written as a fund-raiser for a kindergarten in San Francisco, the first free kindergarten in the West.

Kate Douglas Wiggin was born in Philadelphia in 1856 and spent her childhood in New England. At the tender age of twelve, young Kate met the great Charles Dickens, author of *A Christmas Carol* (1843). The author made a powerful impression on Kate and she later dedicated herself to writing her own novels with a decidedly "Dickensian" flavor, filled with loveable characters and marked by a social conscience mixed with humor. Perhaps her most popular novel was *Rebecca of Sunnybrook Farm* (1903).

Kate came to southern California with her family as a teenager and soon enrolled in a kindergarten training class. In

those days, kindergartens were a new idea, part of a movement to help the inner city's underprivileged youngsters. In 1878 she opened the doors of her own kindergarten on Silver Street in San Francisco. The school was a great success and attracted many distinguished visitors, including the poet Joaquin Miller. He wrote in the school's guest book that visitors touring California should "see the Yosemite Valley first and then the Silver Street Kindergarten!"

To raise money for her fledgling school, Kate Wiggin published *The Birds' Christmas Carol*. The book is a wonderful story to read during the holidays, but readers should be forewarned that it does have a sad ending. The enchanting heroine of the novel is Carol Bird, a sweet, bedridden little girl with a generous soul and an active mind who was born on Christmas Day. She decides to write a story about living alone in her room and the many ways she's found to amuse herself. She then sells the story to a magazine and uses her earnings to buy Christmas presents for some of the poor children in town. On the evening of Christmas Day, Carol says good night to her mother, rests her head on her pillow, and waits to hear the children's voices in a choir. As the choir begins to sing, the voices of the children are so clear and pure that they move everyone listening to tears. But has Carol heard the choir sing? "There were tears in many eyes, but not in Carol's. The loving heart had quietly ceased to beat, and the 'wee birdie' in the great house had flown to its 'home nest.' Carol had fallen asleep! I think perhaps, I cannot say, she heard it after all." Thus ends *The Bird's Christmas Carol* by Kate Douglas Wiggin, a precious gift to the children of Silver Street.

Something More ... The Silver Street Kindergarten has long since disappeared. It once stood on San Francisco's Rincon Hill, nearly invisible today beneath the Bay Bridge. A remnant of Silver Street remains but now bears the name Stillman Street. Read Kate Douglas Wiggin's own story in My Garden of Memory *(1923).*

THE JAMES DEAN STORY

Legendary film star James Dean, born in Indiana in 1931, moved to southern California with his family when he was just five years old. He first became interested in acting when his mother built a miniature stage at home and encouraged him to put on his own private productions with dolls. Later he performed in several high school plays and studied drama at the University of California, Los Angeles. His first professional acting job was a Pepsi commercial in which he and a group of teenagers danced around a jukebox. (From the very beginning, James Dean was typecast!) He soon got several bit parts on television, even appearing opposite Ronald Reagan in a "GE Theater" production. One of his first speaking parts was in a film with Charles Coburn in which he got to deliver that immortal line "Hey, Gramps, I'll have a choc malt, heavy on the choc, plenty of milk, four spoons of malt, and two scoops of ice cream...."

James Dean's biggest films were *Rebel Without a Cause* (1955) and *Giant* (1956) both of which were released after his death. In *Rebel*, he and Natalie Wood and Sal Mineo perfected an image of adolescent alienation that came to be the hallmark of the next decade. His other major film was the screen adaptation of John Steinbeck's *East of Eden* (1955), for which he won an Oscar nomination. His director, Elia Kazan, wasn't all that impressed. "Directing James Dean was like directing Lassie," Kazan complained. "I either lectured him or terrorized him, flattered him furiously...or kicked his backside!"

James Dean had two passions in life, acting and racing sports cars. He was forbidden to do any racing while he was under contract with Warner Brothers for the filming of *Giant*, but as soon as the shooting was over, he bought a new Porsche and headed up to a race in Salinas. He was just east of Paso Robles, travelling over ninety miles an hour, when he crashed on September 30, 1955. It was said that every bone in his body was broken. His death at age twenty-four was front-page news all around the world, and his fans (just like those of Elvis Presley twenty years later) couldn't believe he was really dead. One tabloid even offered a $50,000 reward for information leading to the location of James Dean, believed to be alive and in hiding because his face had been so mangled by the accident. The tabloid's appeal was both heartless and poignant: "Your fans love you--will always love you--no matter what you look like!"

Something More ... Read David Dalton's biography, James Dean, the Mutant King *(1983). Rent a video of one of James Dean's classics; especially recommended is* Rebel Without A Cause. *Also visit the monument at the site of his fatal crash in San Luis Obispo County. It's in the town of Cholame, where State Route 41 meets State Route 46. The inscription says the monument "stands for James Dean and other American Rebels who taught us the importance of having a cause."*

A British View of Monterey

Vancouver, Canada? Yes. Vancouver, Washington? Yes, again. Vancouver, California? Nope, but there ought to be! The great British naval captain George Vancouver explored the California coast between 1792 and 1794, completing with great precision one of the most difficult maritime surveys ever undertaken.

George Vancouver entered the Royal Navy when he was just thirteen years old. He sailed with Captain James Cook on his early voyages to the Pacific and soon rose through the ranks. In 1791 he was given his own command to lead an exploratory voyage around the world. He sailed from England aboard the HMS *Discovery*, rounding the Cape of Good Hope on his way to Australia, Tahiti, and Hawaii. His first sighting of North America's west coast was on April 17, 1792. Vancouver put in at the bays of San Diego, Monterey, and San Francisco in a land he insisted on calling "New Albion," emphasizing its discovery by his countryman, Francis Drake.

Captain Vancouver was especially impressed by the beauty of Monterey. He dropped anchor in the bay on November 26, 1792, and described the land as "a sandy heath...agreeably broken by hills and valleys, with a verdant appearance, and adorned with many clumps and single trees, mostly of the pine tribe, holly-leaved oak, and willows." He marvelled, too, at the "perpetual spring" of Monterey and was amazed to find gardens filled with fresh peas, beans, lettuce, and cabbage. The climate, he remarked, "has the reputation of being as healthy as any part of the known world."

George Vancouver found the Spanish-speaking colonists of Monterey to be quite charming. They were a "generous people, each of whom endeavored to surpass the other in manifesting an interest in our welfare." In appreciation, he hosted a dinner party on board his ship, but his guests soon began to feel a little queasy. "The motion of the ship, though very inconsiderable, greatly to my disappointment, obliged the ladies, and indeed some of the gentlemen, very soon to retire." A couple of nights later, he had more success with a party on the beach. There was a delicious meal "which was not ended until a late hour," dancing, and a display of fireworks that "afforded a very high degree of satisfaction, not only to our visitors, but their dependents of every description." (Say, do you suppose this was what inspired all those great beach-party movies starring Frankie Avalon and Annette Funicello?)

The words of this British traveller ring true today, two hundred years later, for he described California as a beautiful land blessed with a marvelous climate, and filled with friendly people who love to party. A good place to visit, a great place to live!

Something More ... Visit the Monterey Presidio Museum, Corporal Ewing Road, Presidio of Monterey, Monterey 93940. Free. Hours are 1:00 P.M. to 4:00 P.M. Monday through Friday, and 10:00 A.M. to 3:00 P.M. Saturday (closed Sunday). Telephone (408) 647-5414. The words of George Vancouver can be found in Marguerite Wilbur (ed.), Vancouver in California, 1792-1794 *(1953).*

DR. HISTORY'S
HISTORICAL SITES
AND MUSEUMS

INDEX

G

Gabrielino (Indians), 14
"GE Theater," 98
Geddes, Paul, 11
Genoa, Italy, 5, 39
Ghirardelli Square, 39
Ghirardelli, Dominico, 39
Giannini, Amadeo Peter, 39
Giant, 99
Gigling Reservation, 73
Glen Ellen, 81
Glory, 64
gold mining, 28-29, 34, 74, 76-77
gold rush, 1, 6, 10, 12, 34, 38,
    44, 66, 67, 76- 77, 82, 86, 90-
    91
Goldberg, Reuben Lucius
    ("Rube"), 68-69
Golden Era, 90
Golden Gate, 34, 40
Golden Hind , 54
Golden State Warriors, 60
Gomez, José, 72
Grand Canal, Venice, 33
Graz, Austria, 75
Great Seal of the State of
    California, 1-3
Greeley, Horace, 61
Green, Talbot H., 10-11
Greenwich Village, New York,
    33
Greece, 47
grizzly bear, 60-61, 82

H

Hall of Fame, Baseball, 85
Hancock, John, 68
Hancock Park, Los Angeles, 48
Hangtown (Placerville), 12-13
Hangtown Fry, 12-13
Harte, Bret, 76, 90-91

Harvard Lampoon, 84
Harvard University, 84-85
Hastings Law School, 53
Hawaii, 34-35, 40, 100
Hawaiians, 34-35
Hearst, William Randolph, 84-85
Hitler, Adolph, 51
hog wallows, 80-81
Hollywood, 75
Hoover, Herbert, President, 62
Hopkins, Mark, 13
Hopper, William de Wolf , 85
Huntington, Collis P., 13

I

"I Left My Heart in San Francis
    co," 92
Illinois, 94
India, 26
Indiana, 13, 98
Indians, 32, 48, 50-51, 54, 80
    (*see also* names of individual
    tribes)
Inglenook Vineyards, 6
inventions, 68-69
Inyo County, 22-23
Iowa, 52
Irish Americans, 44
Isle of Capri, 38
Italian-Swiss Colony Winery, 39
Italians, 38-39
Italy, 5, 32-33, 38-39, 92
Iwo Jima, 51

J

Japanese Americans, 22-23
Japanese, 41, 50-51
Jeans, 4-5
"Jeopardy" (television program),
    57

Write to Dr. History!

Jim Rawls welcomes your letters.
You can reach him at:
Department of History
Diablo Valley College
Pleasant Hill, CA   94523

Hear more great California
stories with Dr. History on the
SNP RADIO NETWORK.
To find him in your city, call toll free
1-800-578-0750

OTHER BOOKS BY JIM RAWLS

California: An Interpretive History
(New York: McGraw-Hill, Inc., Sixth edition, 1993)
ISBN 0-07-004269-1

> This lively and provocative history of California offers a remarkable balance of narration and interpretation. It includes an unparalleled account of contemporary California, including the fast-paced events of the late 1980s and '90s.

New Directions in California History:
A Book of Readings
(New York: McGraw-Hill, Inc., 1988)
ISBN 051253-1

> Organized chronologically, this book covers a wide range of topics in the social, political, cultural and economic history of the state.